Prepared by the Special Publications Division
National Geographic Society, Washington, D. C.

ALASKA'S MAGNIFICENT
PARKLANDS

ALASKA'S MAGNIFICENT PARKLANDS

Contributing Authors: TOM MELHAM, MARGARET E.
    MURIE, CYNTHIA RUSS RAMSAY, JAMES A. SUGAR
Contributing Photographers: GEORGE HERBEN, JAMES
    H. KATZ, STEPHEN J. KRASEMANN, JAMES A. SUGAR,
    TIM THOMPSON
Published by THE NATIONAL GEOGRAPHIC SOCIETY
    GILBERT M. GROSVENOR, President
    MELVIN M. PAYNE, Chairman of the Board
    OWEN R. ANDERSON, Executive Vice President
    ROBERT L. BREEDEN, Vice President,
    Publications and Educational Media
Prepared by THE SPECIAL PUBLICATIONS DIVISION
    DONALD J. CRUMP, Editor
    PHILIP B. SILCOTT, Associate Editor
    WILLIAM L. ALLEN, WILLIAM R. GRAY,
    Senior Editors
Staff for this Book
    SEYMOUR L. FISHBEIN, Managing Editor
    CHARLES E. HERRON, Picture Editor
    CINDA ROSE, Art Director
    JODY BOLT, Consulting Art Director
    SALLIE M. GREENWOOD, Senior Researcher
    STEPHEN J. HUBBARD, Researcher
    LESLIE ALLEN, PAMELA A. BLACK, RICHARD M.
        CRUM, TONI EUGENE, CHRISTINE ECKSTROM LEE,
        TOM MELHAM, H. ROBERT MORRISON, CATHERINE
        O'NEILL, CYNTHIA RUSS RAMSAY, GENE S. STUART,
        MERRILL WINDSOR, Picture Legend Writers
    JOHN D. GARST, JR., PETER J. BALCH, ROBERT W.
        NORTHROP, JOSEPH F. OCHLAK, JUDITH BELL SIEGEL,
        Map Research, Design, and Production
    REBECCA BITTLE JOHNS, CAROL ROCHELEAU CURTIS,
        Illustrations Assistants
    IVAN K. KING, JENNIFER WOODS, Assistant Designers
Engraving, Printing, and Product Manufacture
    ROBERT W. MESSER, Manager
    GEORGE V. WHITE, Production Manager
    DAVID V. SHOWERS, Production Project Manager
    MARK R. DUNLEVY, GREGORY STORER, GEORGE J.
        ZELLER, JR., Assistant Production Managers;
        MARY A. BENNETT, Production Assistant;
        JULIA F. WARNER, Production Staff Assistant
    NANCY F. BERRY, PAMELA A. BLACK, MARY F.
        BRENNAN, LORI E. DAVIE, MARY ELIZABETH DAVIS,
        CLAIRE M. DOIG, JANET A. DUSTIN, ROSAMUND
        GARNER, VICTORIA D. GARRETT, NANCY J. HARVEY,
        SANDRA K. HUHN, JOAN HURST, ARTEMIS S.
        LAMPATHAKIS, KATHERINE R. LEITCH, MARY
        EVELYN McKINNEY, CLEO E. PETROFF, TAMMY
        PRESLEY, SHERYL A. PROHOVICH, KATHLEEN T.
        SHEA, VIRGINIA A. WILLIAMS, Staff Assistants
    MICHAEL G. YOUNG, Indexer

*Chink in Lake Clark's mountain divide, the cloud-
strewn Merrill Pass area provides a conduit for
flights from Anchorage and nearby towns; one pilot
likened the route to "flying into the mouth of a
shark." PRECEDING PAGES: At Glacier Bay sunset fires
the sky behind the Fairweather Range. PAGE 1:
Prickly rose blooms amid spindly horsetail.
HARDCOVER: Willow ptarmigan, Alaska's state bird.*

Lone hiker traverses Sable Mountain in Denali—where wildlife, extensive visitor facilities, and the crowning glory of Mount McKinley combine to produce Alaska's most popular parkland.

6

CONTENTS

TOM BEAN

INTRODUCTION
THE GREAT COUNTRY

By Margaret E. Murie

HERE IS ELLA HIGGINSON, writing in 1908: "The spell of Alaska falls upon every lover of beauty who has voyaged along those far northern snow-pearled shores with the violet waves of the North Pacific Ocean breaking splendidly upon them; or who has drifted down the mighty rivers of the interior which flow, bell-toned and lonely, to the sea.

"I know not how the spell is wrought," wrote this world traveler in *Alaska: The Great Country,* "nor have I ever met one who could put the miracle of its working into words. No writer has ever described Alaska; no one writer ever will; but each must do his share, according to the spell that the country casts upon him."

Here, in 1982, are the words of a young woman in a letter to me after her first trip to the great country: "Words fail me utterly when I think of Alaska. . . . You should not worry, if you ever do, about whether Alaska is able still to cast the spell on people. It can. It did. The thought that someday it might no longer be able to is more than I can bear. Indeed, it must be preserved for all people, for all time."

Seventy-four years—1908 to 1982. The dates very nearly span the years of my own awareness of Alaska. I grew up in Fairbanks, and when I look back now on my childhood I realize how matter-of-factly we took that life and that great country. There was the town, ticking away with its gold-seeking, love-seeking, society-seeking doings, and thinking very little about the vast wilderness. It was out there somewhere. Lone prospectors disappeared in it. During the summer the stern-wheel steamers came churning up the Chena River with supplies. During the winter the only lifelines were the four- or six-horse sleighs operating between Fairbanks and Valdez. They brought the mail, passengers wrapped in wolfskin robes with charcoal warmers at their feet, and whatever amount of fresh eggs and apples and other lovely things they could manage in the load.

The little town of a few thousand pursued a very full life-style: work or school, dog races, cutter races, snowshoe trips, dog mushing, parties and dinners and club meetings and many, many dances. In summer, the boating-camping trips, berrying, tennis, and baseball (with always the midnight ball game on the 21st of June).

How often did we think about that enormous land? We schoolchildren once a year, perhaps, on Alaska Day, October 18th, when we sang "Alaska, My Alaska" to the tune of "Maryland, My Maryland" and were told that we had been bought from Russia for $7,200,000,

Summer's brief triumph gladdens the icy realm of Wrangell-St. Elias with white yarrow and sprays of squirreltail. Margaret Murie has known Alaska's beauty, winter and summer, since 1911. She and her late husband, Olaus (above, newly wed in 1924), studied the land and its wildlife, joining their work to the conservation movement.

ABOVE: JACK WARWICK
OPPOSITE: STEPHEN J. KRASEMANN

9

and that the Territory of Alaska was divided into four judicial divisions, and that ours, the fourth, was 200,000 square miles in size. But I am sure we were not given the detail published by Sheldon Jackson, the famed missionary, in his 1880 book, *Alaska*: "An area equal to the original thirteen States . . . with the great 'Northwest Territory' added. . . . The shore line up and down the bays and around the islands . . . measures twenty-five thousand miles."

After World War I the government railroad between Anchorage and Fairbanks was built and big mining companies arrived in our interior; our town was greatly enlivened. And in those postwar years came the airplane, which more than any other thing has made life

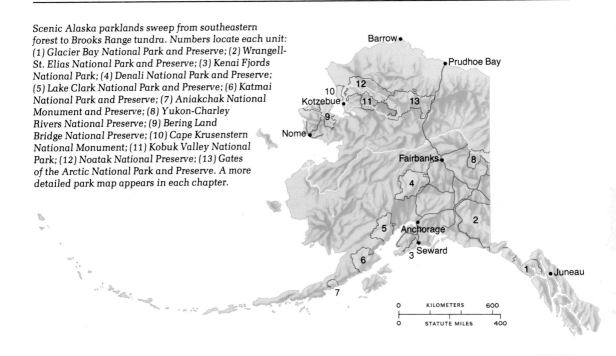

Scenic Alaska parklands sweep from southeastern forest to Brooks Range tundra. Numbers locate each unit: (1) Glacier Bay National Park and Preserve; (2) Wrangell-St. Elias National Park and Preserve; (3) Kenai Fjords National Park; (4) Denali National Park and Preserve; (5) Lake Clark National Park and Preserve; (6) Katmai National Park and Preserve; (7) Aniakchak National Monument and Preserve; (8) Yukon-Charley Rivers National Preserve; (9) Bering Land Bridge National Preserve; (10) Cape Krusenstern National Monument; (11) Kobuk Valley National Park; (12) Noatak National Preserve; (13) Gates of the Arctic National Park and Preserve. A more detailed park map appears in each chapter.

different in Alaska. On a March day in 1924 Carl Ben Eielson took off on one of the first mail flights, Fairbanks southwest to McGrath. My fiancé, Olaus Murie, a government biologist, had left Fairbanks two weeks earlier by dog team on a scientific expedition. Ben made the 270-mile flight and flew home before dark. Olaus didn't reach McGrath until the next day—but he found at the roadhouse a box of my homemade fudge, delivered by air!

The preservation of Alaska's natural splendors in national parkland began in 1917, with the creation of Mount McKinley National Park, today called Denali. A year later Katmai's volcanic wonderland was designated a national monument. And in 1925 Calvin Coolidge, heeding the pleas of science, proclaimed Glacier Bay a national monument of scenic and ecological treasure.

The federal government continued to own most of Alaska. When the territory became a state in 1959, it received 104 million federal acres. Eskimo, Aleut, and Indian people lodged ancestral claims, and in 1971 another 44 million acres were set aside for Native ownership, in addition to a cash payment of nearly a billion dollars. What to do with the rest of Alaska? The struggle to decide continued through the 1970s, and I was happy to play a part.

I had thought I knew something about Alaska: seven trips up and down the southeastern coastline, and 700 miles by dog team in the Koyukuk country of the Brooks Range on my honeymoon. All this had been crowned by two memorable summers on the Sheenjek River. In 1946 Olaus had left the government to become Director of the Wilderness Society; exploring the Sheenjek country of the Brooks Range and working toward its designation as the Arctic National Wildlife Range was the high point of his years at the Society.

And yet, after all this, when I went back north in 1975 as a consultant for the National Park Service, I found there are other worlds in Alaska, other whole ecosystems: the surpassingly beautiful Lake Clark country, the unbelievable Harding Icefield, Cape Krusenstern and its saga of human cultures, living and past.

The future of those worlds lay in the balance as the nation debated the disposition of Alaska lands. The decision came in 1980, and it was an unprecedented triumph for conservation. The Alaska National Interest Lands Conservation Act added some 43.6 million acres to the National Park System, more than doubling its size. Alaska's scenic national parklands, the subject of this book, now number 13: Katmai, Glacier Bay, and Denali—enlarged and sharing national park status—and ten new units. There are also two national historical parks, Sitka and Klondike Gold Rush, which preserve mementos of Russian and Native lifeways and of the great gold stampede of 1897-98. In addition to the parks the landmark law of 1980 dedicated 57 million acres to the national forests and wildlife refuges; 25 streams were added to the National Wild and Scenic Rivers System.

All I can say now is that Alaska is indeed indescribable. Words cannot tell it. Pictures help—but they cannot convey the sense of space, the silence and the sounds, the sounds that belong there: bird song, wolf song, river song. And the air, the skies, the endless light of summer, the soft dark of winter, the feeling of absolute and deep-rooted "selfhood" of pristine untouched country.

Thinking also of the devoted, persistent lovers of that land, who labored through ten years to preserve it, we can proudly say that surely no great expanse of country anywhere ever had such love and energy expended in its behalf.

There is still much to be done. Over the centuries the people of Alaska have evolved a rich tradition of subsisting on the short seasons of bounty in a harsh wilderness. By law, subsistence continues in most of the parklands. There is also provision for sport hunting in designated areas. As you will see in the pages that follow, there is great concern over such provisions, how they will ultimately affect the treasured life-styles of Alaskans—as well as the treasure of parklands that belong to all Americans.

Will we have the wisdom, the courage, the determination to allow this land to keep its primal character? Perhaps young Tony Robinson said it best, speaking for his sixth-grade class at a congressional hearing in Atlanta in 1977: "And I want to add that I, personally, would rather enjoy nature, not remember it."

I remember. I enjoy. And I hope that the sixth graders of the future will be able to enjoy, and to look back and be proud of their countrymen, who gave them a great gift.

ALASKA PARKS ARE DIFFERENT

BIGGER, WILDER, sheltering spectacular arrays of animal life—whales and waterfowl, and grizzlies in goodly numbers—the Alaska national parklands stand out from those in the lower 48. Their very wildness implies other differences. While a few offer the familiar park facilities, most have no roads, no visitor centers, no campgrounds. Rangers are far from plentiful; the permanent staff averages out to one ranger for every 2,312 square miles. Even with an added sprinkling of seasonal rangers, it may be easier to find a bear than a Smokey Bear hat.

Camping is primitive, self-sufficiency the rule. There is challenge and great personal reward for those who can go it alone, but remote bush is probably not the place for novice backpackers without wilderness-seasoned companions. A large variety of travel and tour services, some quite costly, are available through companies, private guides, and outfitters—from plush cruise ships to river running, from sightseeing buses to custom-tailored itineraries by air charter. For information on such services write the Regional Director, National Park Service, 2525 Gambell Street, Anchorage, Alaska 99503, or Alaska State Division of Tourism, Pouch E, Juneau, Alaska 99811. Conservation groups such as the Sierra Club also schedule outings.

Some 33.1 million acres of Alaska parkland have been placed in the National Wilderness Preservation System. In the lower 48 the system forbids motorized travel except where specifically authorized. In Alaska, just the opposite: Snowmobiles, motorboats, and airplanes are acceptable anywhere they're not specifically banned.

Outside of Alaska the national parks, with minor exceptions, ban hunting. But many Alaskans are devoted sport hunters, and not a few have an important economic stake in guiding outsiders who yearn for a shot at the majestic animals of the northern wilds. In consequence, large chunks of Alaska parklands, including three entire units, have been designated as national preserves, which allow sport hunting. The state regulates it; to hunt Dall's sheep and brown bears, out-of-state citizens must be with guides or relatives who live in Alaska. The Park Service is charged with preventing the depletion of the resource. There is also commercial trapping in the preserves. Alaska's waters are a fisherman's paradise, and all the parklands are open to sport fishing; a state license is required.

Native people and others in a category of so-called local and rural residents are entitled to continue established patterns of living off the land: hunting, fishing, trapping, cropping berries, downing wood for fuel and shelter. Natives may take walrus ivory for handicrafts. The subsistence privilege applies in all units except the national park areas of Katmai, Kenai Fjords, Glacier Bay, and pre-1980 Denali.

Though today's technology has decreased the necessity for subsistence living, Natives—with support from many conservationists—insist on the right to pursue the traditions of their forefathers. In so doing they preserve the strategies and techniques of survival in one of the cruelest of climes. Such living archives can provide a rich experience to visitors. But park authorities urge respect for the privacy of people living in the parks. It is their right to welcome, or not.

Respect for the land and the people, and the goal of a safe and enjoyable visit suggest a check with park headquarters before planning a trip. In the chapters that follow, the map pages contain addresses for each park, as well as details on facilities and access.

Snows of yesteryear linger on the slopes in Kenai Fjords, where mile-high mountains hem the wild coast. One gravel road touches a corner of Kenai; most visitors glimpse the fjords and the adjacent offshore wildlife from boats—including state ferries. Roadlessness typifies Alaska parklands; special rules allow air taxis and charters into much of the wilderness.

GEORGE HERBEN

GLACIER BAY

By Cynthia Russ Ramsay

A CHILL MIST hung over the snowy mountains and the smooth water where harbor seals dozed on icebergs drifting in the tide and currents of the sea. Ahead, at the end of the narrow inlet, loomed the Johns Hopkins Glacier, a river of ice rippled with dark ribbons of pulverized rock. From time to time a violent crack rent the silence as a slab weighing hundreds of tons broke off the glacier's 200-foot-high face and crashed into the depths in a geyser of spray.

Ice thundering into the sea and spectacular fjords have astounded visitors to Glacier Bay for a century. So many, including scientists, fell under its spell that it was declared a national monument in 1925. Under the landmark conservation law of 1980 the bay and its surroundings were redesignated a national park and preserve.

On the 55-mile flight from park headquarters at Bartlett Cove to Johns Hopkins Inlet my guide Greg Streveler and I traversed the full length of Glacier Bay—passing from the lushness of a rain forest to land scraped bare by ice. Heading northwest above the watery corridor, we had skirted a trackless domain—a wilderness for wolves, for mountain goats pirouetting across stony ridges, for brown bears flopped down in beach meadows, gorging on strawberries. Directly below us waters rich in plankton, shrimp, and fish attracted killer whales, porpoises, and the most cherished summer visitors—the humpback whales, whose mysterious decline in recent years has perplexed scientists and troubled park officials.

The bay's fertile waters also brought thousands upon thousands of birds. Wherever we looked birds were on the move. A flock of dainty red-necked phalaropes landed weightlessly on the water. Tufted puffins, plump black birds with orange-and-yellow parrot beaks, dived into the bay as deep as a hundred feet, and common mergansers took to the air with a furious beating of wings.

The floatplane landed in the fjord and left us to wade ashore on a rocky beach, where we were surrounded by the Fairweather Range, its heights ascending into the clouds with stunning abruptness. As soon as Greg assembled the two-seat collapsible kayak, we paddled deeper into the mile-wide fjord. Occasionally clouds parted and the full immensity of a sharp-cut peak, pale and luminous, filled the gap.

On our left the Kashoto and Hoonah Glaciers spilled down between granite ridges to the edge of the sea. Other, smaller pockets of ice were impounded above the near-vertical rock walls. From these hanging glaciers water cascaded down in slender, silvery columns.

Bright as a flame, a skiers' tent emblazons crevasse-torn Brady Glacier, wending seaward under a grimy coat of morainal debris and landslide. Above it, like streams feeding a lake, tributary glaciers flow into the park's largest icefield. Here in southeast Alaska, plant life—from shy maiden flowers (above) to spruce forest—reclaims the land as the glaciers shrink.

GLACIER BAY NATIONAL PARK AND PRESERVE. 3,234,000 acres. MAJOR FEATURES: Glaciers on the move, changing plant communities, land and marine mammals, seabirds. FACILITIES: Information station, campground, tour boats, hiking trails. ACCESS AND ACCOMMODATIONS: Air service to Gustavus; boat service, air and boat charters to park; lodging in park and Gustavus; supplies at Gustavus. ACTIVITIES: Bay and fjord touring by cruise vessel and kayak to observe birds, mammals, calving glaciers; backpacking, climbing, cross-country skiing on glaciers; river running, fishing. Sport hunting in preserve. FOR INFORMATION: Superintendent, Bartlett Cove, Gustavus, Alaska 99826.

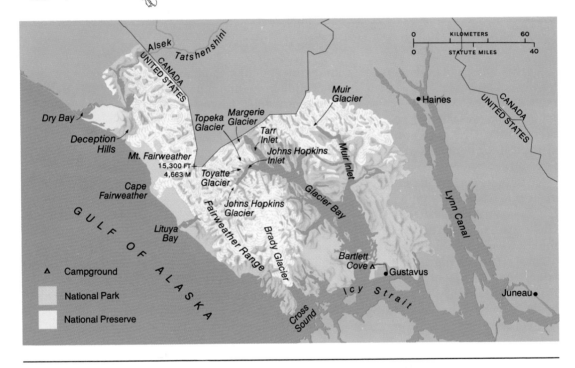

On the other shore the Topeka and Toyatte Glaciers had receded up the valleys of their own making, leaving moraine deposits—boulders, gravel, and fine sediment shaped into slopes of rubble. Over the years melt from the glaciers had channeled down these slopes. Scattered across the somber gray debris were small plants bright with the colors of September—yellow arctic willows, ruby dwarf fireweed, and cottony tufts of mountain avens gone to seed.

"Look! Every time a glacier backs away, life just charges into the void, and the land again erupts with greenery and song," exclaimed Greg, a biologist who has worked for the Park Service and has spent much of the last 15 years exploring and studying Glacier Bay. He provided me with a simplified summary of the stages by which life returns to these barren shores—a sequence that has created a spruce and hemlock forest around Bartlett Cove in less than 200 years.

"The process scientists call plant succession," he said, "begins primarily with tundra plants—mosses, dwarf fireweed, horsetails, and mountain avens, which can take root in rock crevices or find footholds in the loose gravel. Seedlings of alders, willows, and cottonwoods get started then also. These shrubby species eventually form dense thickets that shade out the other pioneers. But the thickets harbor young spruces that in time form another, higher canopy: the spruce forest. And spruces in turn are eventually outnumbered by hemlocks whose young can thrive in the deep shade of the forest floor when the spruces cannot. All the while, decaying plants and animal droppings are helping to build soil on the infertile surface. Johns Hopkins, with its severe weather and steep terrain, is a tough place for plants. Perhaps this land will support only thickets, but certainly it won't stay fireweed and mountain avens for long."

Greg's discourse had not interrupted the rhythm of his strokes, and before long ice closed in and bumped and scraped the kayak's sides. "Looks like we'll have to push a little ice to get to our campsite," he said. "But as long as we don't hit the floes dead on the bow, the ice will slide past." As we neared our destination, we maneuvered the kayak onto a dark beach, where tiny icebergs had been stranded at ebb tide. They had melted into graceful shapes, gleaming like glass sculptures before tapering slowly, imperceptibly away.

Near the head of the fjord, where the ice pack is densest, as many as 2,500 harbor seals gather in summer to bear their pups and to mate. Now, in September, many had departed, but from time to time a small, pointed face would bob up out of the water to look us over with bright-eyed curiosity.

Like seals, the humpback whales draw spectators. In fact, the presence of this endangered species has helped increase the park's popularity—from a trickle of 8,000 visitors in 1968 to a flood of 96,500 in 1983. Most view the park from cruise ships and charter boats. And from late May to late September daily boat tours out of Bartlett Cove travel past silent spruce forests, past craggy islands raucous with the cries of birds, to the very edge of an ice age—all in a matter of hours.

One of the most thrilling sights is a humpback breaching—30 or 40 tons of whale catapulting into the air and crashing back into the sea. But even a glimpse of a fluke, or of a spout hanging above the water like a cloud of mist, is a memorable event.

Whales begin to arrive here in June to feed during the summer. In 1978, 19 whales, about the usual number, showed up, but halfway through the season all but three left suddenly. The disappearance coincided with an increase in boat traffic, but no one knows for sure if this caused the abrupt departure.

Charles Jurasz, however, has little doubt. A science teacher in Juneau and a marine researcher, he has been studying Glacier Bay whales since 1966. A boat serves as his home and research vessel. For seven years he worked under Park Service contract. Jurasz is certain the whales are bothered by noisy boats. Some of the arriving whales may have fasted all winter, he says, and in Glacier Bay they eat all the time, swallowing enormous quantities of herring, capelin, shrimp, and small crustaceans known as krill. When a vessel approaches, he adds, the whales may stop feeding and dive or breach or slap the water with their tails or fins. Jurasz concludes that the interruptions became so frequent the whales abandoned the area.

There are others who contend that the humpbacks may have left because of a food shortage, possibly due to a cyclical ebb in production of prey species. In any case the whales became one of the most crucial resource problems in the entire park system. John Chapman, Glacier Bay superintendent at the time, (Continued on page 24)

FOLLOWING PAGES: Frozen waves in a translucent sea highlight the wonder of discovery for a hiker exploring an ice cave near Muir Glacier. Meltwater and temperature change sculptured this natural gallery of art; time and pressure tinted it, producing a dense, crystalline ice that absorbs other hues but reflects the blues. A warming spell can swiftly turn on a torrent—hazard to the spelunker and to the fanciful sculpture.

Beached icebergs surround a kayaker on a 50-mile outing in the park. Maneuvering amid the bergs may require a deft paddle; they flip over, pop up from the seafloor, break apart. But kayakers explore wilderness coves where cruise ships seldom go. Some visitors choose the perspective of an aerial view to enjoy the grandeur, such as Margerie Glacier (left). This thick jumble curls more than 20 miles down from the Fairweather Range; its pinnacled seracs rise 180 feet above the tidewater edge of Tarr Inlet.

responded to the emergency, reducing cruise ship traffic and setting lower speed limits. He also ordered vessels away from the shore, where the whales prefer to feed. A few whales have since returned.

Cruise ship interests fought for greater boat access; environmentalists demanded greater controls. Park Service officials commissioned additional research. The studies initially encountered delay and equipment failure. In mid-1983 the researchers urged a continuation of traffic restrictions until more conclusive data could be gathered. Whether the Park Service can maintain the waters as a summer sanctuary for whales, only time will tell.

Time seems especially dynamic in Glacier Bay. The array of plant life is constantly changing; the glaciers are on the move, retreating on the bay's east side, remaining stable or advancing on the west side; the land itself is rising about an inch and a half a year in the areas where the weight of the ice has been removed.

Two hundred years ago Glacier Bay did not even exist. It lay under a vast sheet of ice up to 4,000 feet thick—the work of a "little ice age" which began some 40 centuries ago. In the 18th century a warming trend started to thaw the glaciers. When British explorer George Vancouver sent boats into Icy Strait in 1794, Glacier Bay was only a dent

in a shoreline of ice. By the time the eloquent naturalist John Muir arrived in 1879, a large bay was waiting to be explored. Muir and others saw Glacier Bay as a unique outdoor laboratory. Geologists came to gain insights into the movements of glaciers. Botanists marveled at tree stumps, relics of forests that had been covered by advancing glaciers and then exposed by their retreat.

Muir's writing and enthusiasm and the work of scientists helped bring fame and more field researchers—and eventually the flotillas of cruise ships—to Glacier Bay. But not many cruise ships take tourists to the park's seldom visited outer coast, where rough surf and Pacific storms brawl with sandy beaches and coastal forests.

A charter plane dropped me on a shore of Lituya Bay—a stunning,

T-shaped basin fronting snowcapped mountains. During a violent earthquake in 1958 about 90 million tons of rock and ice shook loose from the mountains and crashed into the bay. Water shot 1,700 feet high. Now thickets of alder cover the scars—a swath of bright green, in contrast to dark spruce, that hints at the devastation.

From Lituya it is some 50 miles north to Dry Bay, where a salmon processing plant operates within Glacier Bay's newly added preserve. The pilot flew so low we spotted five brown bears in a seaside meadow. Beyond Cape Fairweather we were traveling past the entire northwest addition, 580,000 acres that include the small preserve. It is dazzling country, with the white ramparts of the Fairweathers towering over a narrow coastal plain. The area contains salmon streams, important habitat for bears, wolves, and moose, and protects the Alsek River—popular with river runners for its scenery and challenging rapids. Before long we saw the pale Alsek, heavy with glacial silt, pouring into the dark Pacific. We turned inland and skimmed the gravel delta flamboyant with miles of blooming paintbrush, then bumped to a landing on a Dry Bay gravel strip.

Tlingit Indians from the town of Yakutat fish for the processing plant during salmon season. Some 20 other fishermen are seasonal residents in the preserve under Park Service permit. Like many Alaskans, they are irked by regulations, especially restrictions imposed by the government. But the Indians had fought to keep this land within the federal system—hoping to prevent development that would threaten their traditional hunting and fishing grounds.

A delicate time of transition confronted the Park Service in such newly protected areas as Dry Bay. And for John Cook, Park Service director for the Alaska region, the years just after passage of the Alaska Lands Act brought many political pressures. In 1983 Cook was transferred out of the state. Spokesmen for the Department of the Interior called it a "career enhancement" move; conservationists denounced the transfer as a political purge.

Before Cook was reassigned I talked with him about problems at Dry Bay. "We must be sensitive to the needs of people who are suddenly finding themselves under our jurisdiction," he told me. "The first priority is to establish a park presence without alienating people. We're trying to avoid confrontations. With patience and persistence, I think we'll be able to work conflicts out."

Backcountry Ranger Richard Steele, an engaging young man with an ability to soothe irate tempers, sought to apply these policies at Dry Bay. The day I arrived he had spent the morning listening to a resident sound off about the need for building permits. "Actually some are rushing to put buildings up without one because they know we're treading lightly at this stage," Richard told me.

One change did go into effect. For years as many as 30 bears had been scavenging the wastes of the processing plant. The Park Service, determined to reestablish natural conditions for wildlife, ordered the garbage buried inside an electric fence. The bears countered by trying to dig under the fence, and residents complained of bears damaging fishnets and gear in the hunt for food.

It will take a little time for the bears to forget about the handouts. It may take even longer to resolve the conflicts between human use and protecting the wilderness. But a start has been made: to let the scars heal, to favor nature's way, in Dry Bay, as in the rest of the park.

Sharp-eyed food shopper, a bald eagle grasps carrion in its talons on a berg calved from Muir Glacier. In spring, when harbor seals haul out to bear pups on the icy islands, eagles feed on protein-rich afterbirth. The bergs also offer fishing perches to eagles and cormorants. Since we see only the tips of icebergs, how much lies below? Up to nine-tenths, scientists say, depending on density of the berg and water salinity. Some Alaskans mix drinks with berg ice; as it melts, bubbles pop, adding a natural fizz.

M eadow palette of Indian paintbrush borders the Alsek River, part of the half-million-acre addition to the parkland. A storied white water stream, the Alsek cuts a valley through which moose, bears, and wolves gain access to rich habitat along the Gulf of Alaska coast.

FOLLOWING PAGES: *"The . . . chaste and spiritual heights,"* wrote John Muir of the Fairweather Range, *whose tallest summit, Mount Fairweather, towers 15,300 feet. The vista spans more than 50 miles from Muir Inlet, named for the naturalist who popularized Glacier Bay. Near here he built a cabin at the foot of Muir Glacier; in the century since, the glacier has retreated 20 miles.*

"Thar she blows!" A humpback whale sprays a misty spout as breath rushing from a nostril, or blowhole, meets colder outside air and condenses. Humpbacks feed in Glacier Bay through the summer—but their numbers have dropped off. Concern for this endangered species, whose North Pacific population may total a thousand or so, has brought restrictions on vessel traffic in the park—and controversy. Most musically gifted of sea mammals, humpbacks sing haunting melodies that can last 30 minutes. Observers have also heard a brassy whistling when the whales inhale.

WILLIAM BOEHM

R ain forest reborn:
Spruces and hemlocks
near a Bartlett Cove trail
(opposite) shade land
that lay under ice 200
years ago. Diverse flora
adapted to the changing
environment, each kind
in its time and favored
site: Fern grows in
shade, skunk cabbage
(left) in bogland.
Spruces replaced alders,
but the future belongs to
hemlocks. And as ice
recedes, the unburdened

land springs up—at the
rate of $1\frac{1}{2}$ inches a year.
So the drama of Glacier
Bay continues: the
quaking of mountains,
the thunder of glaciers,
and the gentle triumph
of the forest.

WRANGELL-SAINT ELIAS

By Cynthia Russ Ramsay

SUPERLATIVES BEGIN TO TELL THE STORY of Wrangell-Saint Elias National Park and Preserve. Its size alone staggers the imagination: 13.2 million acres, almost six Yellowstones in extent. The largest of all national parks contains the highest coastal mountains and four of the fifteen highest peaks in North America. Its glaciers, and there are hundreds, perhaps thousands of them, count among the longest, largest, and most active anywhere. On its high, treeless slopes and precipitous ridges dwell some of the world's finest herds of Dall's sheep, prized by trophy hunters for their long, curling horns. Its rock, born of volcanic fires and sediments formed at the bottom of the sea, harbors rich veins of ore that have yielded millions of dollars in silver and gold and produced a billion pounds of copper.

There is also an immensity of beauty: in the deep gorges of the Chitistone and Kotsina Rivers, where each stratum of rock smolders with a different color; in the august grandeur of Mount St. Elias soaring mightily from the edge of the sea 18,008 feet into the sky; in a flock of trumpeter swans gliding regally across the quiet waters of the lower Bremner River; and in the solitary lynx that steals through the forest and deep snows on wide, padded paws.

From the Copper River in the west the park-preserve sprawls eastward in a tumult of peaks to the Canadian border. The Chugach and the St. Elias ranges sweep the southern rim, bordering on the Gulf of Alaska. Wedged between heights of the Chugach Mountains, the Bagley Icefield stretches for 80 miles in a terrible emptiness. In the north, beyond the crescent of the Wrangells and the contiguous University Range, rise the Mentastas and Nutzotins, part of the mighty Alaska Range. These northern flanks taper into Tanana River lowlands daubed with myriad lakes and ponds.

About 80 percent of the park is high country of snow, rock, and ice—uninhabited and, in places, still unexplored. I went to such a place with Gunnar Naslund, a young attorney who virtually abandoned law for the mountains, becoming a licensed guide and climbing instructor. Our pilot was Paul Claus, who at 22 had more than eight years' experience flying in the bush.

On a brilliant July morning, with the sun flaring on the fuzzy blooms of cotton grass and temperatures in the 70s, Paul took off in his Super Cub from a gravel bar on the Chitina. A glacial river, the Chitina pours out of the St. Elias Mountains and weaves a rambling, braided course between the Chugach and the Wrangells before it

With a thunderous splash 25 stories high, a pinnacle of ice calves from 70-mile-long Hubbard Glacier. Though ice smothers much of Wrangell-St. Elias, the world's largest national park, forested valleys and flowered meadows count among its scenic delights.

TOM BEAN

35

WRANGELL-SAINT ELIAS NATIONAL PARK AND PRESERVE. 13,188,000 acres. MAJOR FEATURES: Largest unit in the National Park System; contains some of the world's longest, largest glaciers, North America's largest concentration of high peaks. Wild rivers and canyons; wildlife. FACILITIES: Park office near Copper Center; hiking routes. ACCESS AND ACCOMMODATIONS: Rough roads to McCarthy and Nabesna. Bus service to Glennallen. Air service to some perimeter towns; air charters into park. Lodging along perimeter and at Yakutat; some private lodgings in park (write for list). ACTIVITIES: Backpacking, mountaineering, vehicle camping, cross-country skiing, fishing, river running. Sport hunting in preserve. FOR INFORMATION: Superintendent, Box 29, Glennallen, Alaska 99588.

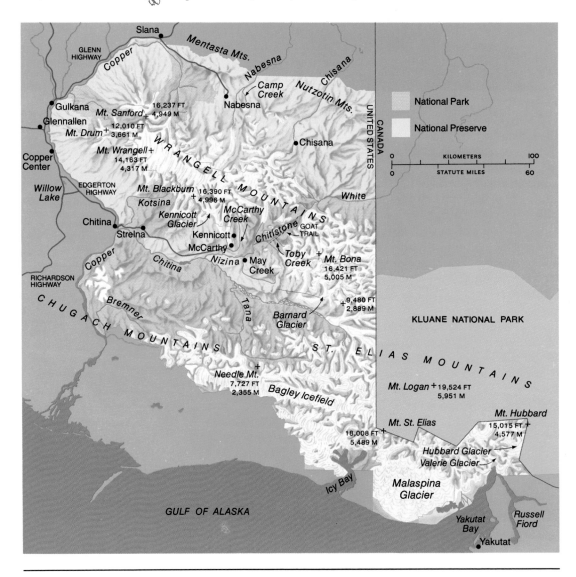

joins the Copper. We flew upstream, heading toward the pure-white mass shimmering on the eastern horizon—Canada's Mount Logan, at 19,524 feet the continent's second highest peak after McKinley. After 20 miles Paul turned northeast to follow the broad avenue of the Barnard Glacier, which ascends into the St. Elias range between snow-veined precipices. All along its length, some 35 miles, tributary glaciers curved sharply into the main flow—the rubble from their valley walls merging into the Barnard to form dark stripes that spoke eloquently of the power of erosion.

As we passed these nameless valleys, I caught glimpses of great snow cornices and shining peaks and cirques brimming with ice—an impregnable landscape in white. "You can't hike into country like this," said Paul. For Paul, as for many Alaskans, a light plane serves as a flying jeep on such terrain. We landed at 6,500 feet on a glacier that swung off the Barnard in a long, gentle rise. To the hollow rumble of snow avalanching down a cliff I stepped out into the dazzling brightness and found myself surrounded by peaks that, as far as my companions were aware, no one had ever climbed before.

Our destination, a summit measured on the topographical map at 9,480 feet, did not seem so far away. It was the rest of the world that seemed utterly distant. When Paul's father flew the plane back to their cabin on the Chitina, we were completely cut off. For me the isolation added an intimidating dimension, one that can surround a visitor almost anywhere in the park. For Gunnar and Paul the solitude and uncertainty embodied the essence of wilderness.

"In true wilderness you have to live by your own resources. You have to take care of yourself and deal with your own mistakes," Gunnar told me. "The possibility of danger heightens your awareness and gives you a closer relationship to the land. When I'm climbing, nothing else exists, and I feel part of the mountain, part of the natural world." Gunnar spoke of these things at rest stops during our seven-hour climb. Our route lay up the glacier and then onto the mountain, where an avalanche had exposed a spillway of glistening ice. Creeping up its 300-foot length, I discovered the crampons strapped to our boots were indeed remarkable tools, particularly when I heeded Gunnar's advice to move with a flat-footed gait, so all the steel points would bite into the ice. "Don't lean into the hill. It levers the points out of the ice," he reminded me again and again.

We had been roped for safety from the start, and on that steep ice we used ice screws. Paul in the lead pounded and twisted a giant steel screw into the ice and so anchored our rope to the mountain. Then we progressed in slow stages, advancing 30 feet or so from one protected point to the next.

Only five days after we stood atop the snow-covered summit, Gunnar attempted another first ascent in the park—7,727-foot Needle Mountain in the Chugach, above the Bagley Icefield. A large cornice above him suddenly broke off. Tons of snow came crashing down and knocked Gunnar from a sheer ice face. His climbing partner was belaying him. The rope arrested Gunnar's fall and held his body above a couloir that plunged several thousand feet. But the snow crushed him against the ice wall, and he died instantly.

No one who ventures among the mountains ever forgets that climbing can be hazardous and unpredictable. But people like Gunnar willingly assume the risks. For those who mourn him there is some consolation in knowing that Gunnar would have chosen to die in the mountains whose beauty he loved so much.

For more than 70 years the huge white volcanoes of the Wrangells, extinct now except for smoking Mount Wrangell, have spurred climbers to feats of skill and endurance. An early success in the range came in 1912. Dora Keen of Philadelphia, five feet tall and 40 years

old, started up 16,390-foot Mount Blackburn with seven men. Six gave up; she and the seventh, a prospector who later became her husband, made it to the top, surviving 22 days in snow caves with only candles to melt water for tea.

Even cross-country travel is arduous and sometimes dangerous because of steep terrain, swift streams, dense brush, and the possibility of snow at any time of the year at higher elevations. But neither hazard nor hardship deterred the prospectors who stormed up into the Wrangells in the late 1800s and early 1900s. Some found their way over the mountains on the Chitistone Goat Trail.

This historic trail, used for centuries by the Athapaskan Indians, today attracts seasoned backpackers. Dona Agosti, mother of seven and author of the book *The High-Country Backpacker,* considers the trail the most scenic and most challenging in Alaska. In her fifties Dona led a Chitistone trip, flying into one landing strip and out from another 27 miles and 6 days later—a trek that inspired and terrified her. "Our first challenge was wading across Toby Creek, which was rushing along in ten separate channels," she recalled. "A few miles farther the boiling, boulder-rolling, chocolate-brown Chitistone River presented an even greater obstacle. One of the husky six-footers

*Peaceable kingdom:
Wildlife tamely crowds
the Ellis family trophy
room. From his home in
the Wrangells preserve,
where the law permits
hunting, Bill Ellis guides
clients to such prizes as
grizzly, caribou, and
Dall's sheep. More than
a third of the parklands'
54.7 million acres in
Alaska have preserve
status. Not enough, say
hunting groups. Plenty,
say environmentalists.
A broadside (opposite)
in the war of words
employs grim humor
in targeting opponents.*

crossed first, belayed by another big guy; the two established a fixed line onto which each of us clipped our carabiners. Then we hobbled across gripping our staffs with both hands. At one point the trail crossed a steep scree slope that dropped more than 2,000 feet into the gorge of the Chitistone. One look at the trail about 12 inches wide turned my stomach. But we prayed a lot and beat the odds.

"At Chitistone Pass the view of glaciers, peaks, and lakes seemed to go on forever, and the click of our cameras sent the ground squirrels into a chirping frenzy," reported Dona. "We had air access, freeze-dried food, waterproof tents, and Polarguard sleeping bags; the early prospectors had roadhouses, packhorses, and Indian porters. Yet I wonder if we did not share similar moments of fear and equal portions of awe when viewing nature's untamed violence and breathtaking beauty in these Wrangell Mountains."

There was a time, from 1911 to 1938, when visitors could ride a railroad through a part of the Wrangells. A 195-mile track bridged canyons, crossed the Copper River twice, and edged past glaciers—a tremendous engineering feat that took more than four years to complete. Copper was the catalyst; the rails went from the port of Cordova up the Copper and Chitina valleys to the Kennecott mill, which was processing fortunes from mines tunneled into mountains above the company town. But by 1938 it had become a losing business and the mines closed. The trains stopped; Kennicott became an instant ghost town. (Variant spellings of town and mill honor the same man, naturalist Robert Kennicott.) The town's frame buildings, still a deep red from the original paint, stand empty now; machinery rusts in the shops and patients' charts are strewn on the hospital floor. As I rummaged in the silent buildings, the wind sighed through chinks in the walls and a bird warbled by a broken bunkhouse window.

The town is now a private holding within the park, its owners maintaining an interest in copper, real estate development, historic preservation, and a summer science school plan. Some houses of the mining management have been sold and restored as vacation homes.

Copper also created McCarthy, 4½ miles down the valley, where miners once caroused. Today the community counts some 20 year-round residents. They haul water, chop firewood, garden, raise chickens, and fish and hunt. If one person gets a moose, a lot of townsfolk share it. They go to Anchorage once or twice a year to buy staples. Some leave town occasionally to take seasonal jobs.

Ben Shaine and his wife enlarged a cabin, paneling it with hand-planed boards because they didn't want to hear the generator. "Writing about the way we live won't capture the special character of McCarthy," he said. "Instead, encourage people to experience the vastness and power of the landscape that dominates our lives.

"We live in the midst of great geologic forces," he went on. "Glaciers, volcanoes, rampaging rivers that flood and rechannel repeatedly." McCarthy itself is built on a gravel bar that may have been deposited by a few major floods of McCarthy Creek—and could be buried when another major flood recurs.

Someone once insisted that Shaine explain why he had spent so much time in the area. "I finally told him to take a walk 15 miles into the mountains," said Shaine. "Go up McCarthy Creek by starlight at 30 below. Go out and see the land. Go ask a moose."

The community has few links to the outside world, and people like it that way. A mail plane lands at the airstrip once a week. The primitive, unpaved state road from the town of Chitina follows the old railbed for 65 miles across streams, bogs, and ruts until it dead-ends at the Kennicott River, where bridges have washed out.

"To get to McCarthy," explained painter Loy Green, "you must leave your vehicle and pull yourself across on a rickety cable tram. Its slack lines drop the tram low over the river, so it's like pulling yourself uphill." Residents usually park beside the river and fly across to McCarthy with a local pilot—avoiding also a second tram that crosses another channel of the river closer to town. One tram was rebuilt in 1983; the other is scheduled for rebuilding.

The passage of years has graced the scattering of gray frame buildings with a ramshackle charm that makes McCarthy a magnet. But the road discourages visitors, and some townsfolk oppose any upgrading. "Its relative isolation is part of McCarthy's unique culture," asserts one resident. Others, equally adamant, want better access into

Silhouetted against a snowy expanse, a guide and three novice climbers cross Kennicott Glacier. Azure snowmelt fills a gully, adding to the hazards of a summer expedition. At heights where perpetual snow conceals death-trap crevasses, climbers rope up for safety.

the Chitina Valley. ''That tremendous country belongs to everyone,''
they contend. The Park Service, standing somewhere in between,
would like the state road improved so that travel over it does not become a test of man and machinery.

The state holds title to some 20,000 acres near McCarthy and had
planned to subdivide some for private sale. To head off the prospect
of subdivisions within the parkland, the Park Service sought to acquire the tract in exchange for acreage in other parks. As negotiations
dragged on, the idea of a land swap troubled some environmentalists. They welcomed protection for the prime Wrangells tract but saw
a dangerous precedent in letting the state pick and choose from other
prime parklands that had been placed in the system by federal law.

Others also own property in the park—a total of more than 700,000
acres. Huge tracts belonging to the Ahtna Indians checkerboard the
banks of the Copper and Chitina Rivers, and the Chugach Native corporation has rights to enclaves in the pristine 40-mile valley of the

Bremner River and at Icy Bay along the coast. Native properties cannot be acquired without the owner's consent, and Native groups are willing to negotiate. Eventually the Park Service may be able to buy or trade for some of these plots; meanwhile, the Ahtna Native regional corporation has pushed ahead with mineral exploration and with plans to operate copper, gold, and zinc-lead mines.

No one can stake new mining claims in parks or preserves. Mining interests consider this ban in the mineral-rich Wrangells one of the big "lock-ups" of the Alaska parklands law. But old claims are valid and there are more than a thousand of them in the park.

As Congress debated the legislation, hunting interests lobbied

PAUL CLAUS

relentlessly to place prime areas for Dall's sheep in preserves. The resulting compromise put a third of Wrangell-St. Elias in the preserve category—open to sport hunting. The battle goes on. Alaska Senator Ted Stevens has backed a bill to transfer as much as 12 million acres of Alaska parkland into preserves.

Many Alaskans consider hunting an essential ingredient of their life-style and look forward to the yearly take of moose or caribou. In the Wrangells the lure may be a trophy of massive, curling ram's horns. In season Alaskans and hunters from around the world arrive in numbers that make hunting the leading recreational activity in the Wrangells and keep some 50 licensed guides in business. Out-of-staters interested in Dall's sheep or grizzlies are required by law to employ guides who, for a fee—some $4,500 for a full-curl, mature ram, $5,000 for a grizzly—all but guarantee a client a kill. The guide finds the animal and stalks it. The client has only to shoot it. The guide's job may also include getting shot at. It seems some hunters get buck fever when they close in and just start shooting wild.

Bill Ellis, a lean, convivial man whose wind-worn face creases frequently into a smile, has devoted his life to guiding since 1955. "A hunt still starts the adrenaline pumping," he said, speaking in the soft, slurred accents of Texas. Bill invited me to join a hunter camped near the Nabesna River in the northern reaches of the preserve. He had some words of caution about clothes: I could wear any color as long as the clothing had a bold pattern that would break up my silhouette. Mountain sheep have very keen eyesight—hunters believe it is equal to a seven- or eight-power scope.

Scrambling over the bouldery canyon of Camp Creek taught me that there are no flat places when you are stalking Dall's sheep. From time to time we slogged across a slope mantled with spongy turf. "To get in shape for this kind of terrain," said Bill, mopping his brow, "you fill the basement with mattresses and jog."

Every few hundred yards he paused to "glass" the terrain with his binoculars, then waved us on. Suddenly he tensed and turned us toward a rocky niche. As we settled into it, Bill eased up the next rise on his stomach and lay there watching. Finally he returned and hunkered down beside us. He had spotted some ewes upslope.

"No way we could have moved with the three ewes up there," he said. "Now they've gone down into the gully and haven't come back up the other side. Something attracted them. It's bound to be feed or water. Whatever it is, maybe it drew some rams, too. So let's go."

The hunter loaded his 30-06 and set off behind Bill in a crouching lope. Just before we came to the last rise a ewe burst out of the gully. Then five rams went bounding past us uphill. Bill dropped to his knees, pointing and shouting, "That one, that one."

The hunter steadied his rifle on Bill's shoulder. A hard, sharp crack rang out across the canyon. Then a whoop of pure joy. The lead ram was dead, and Bill could say, "We have us another payday."

Bill's knowledge of game makes him a good hunter. He is also a good guide in a profession that—according to state officials and environmentalists—counts some scofflaw members: those who poach, herd game by airplane, and let clients violate the law that bars hunting the same day they are airborne. The Park Service has the chore of policing the sport. "To patrol an area this size," said Bill, "they'd have to put together an air force."

In fact, Superintendent Chuck Budge must watch over a park bigger than Vermont and New Hampshire combined with a permanent staff of 7, plus 11 seasonals. When I spoke about this, he replied, "It's almost impossible to cover the whole park; you manage pieces that you know are being used by visitors. The ice and snow and rocks take care of themselves."

There's been progress since the first year, when Chuck and his rangers—known as "Chuck's huskies" because of their size—bore the brunt of local resentment against the "Feds." In Glennallen, near park headquarters at Copper Center, a service station wouldn't sell them gas. Restaurants wouldn't always serve them. Rangers' lives were threatened. A Park Service plane was set afire.

"The task hasn't been easy," Chuck told me, "but we're getting along with the local people a little better now. We're getting them to listen to our position.

"And, by God, there's nothing to rival this country in all the world. It's worth every effort to safeguard this great wilderness."

KENAI FJORDS

By Cynthia Russ Ramsay

"THE KENAI FJORDS," cautions the Park Service, "are rugged, remote, and exposed to the tempestuous Gulf of Alaska. Strong currents flow past them and few landing sites exist. You are strongly advised to employ an experienced guide and seaworthy craft."

No one is more qualified to ply these waters than Pam Oldow, trim and youthful in her early 50s, and the first woman in Alaska licensed to pilot a vessel on the open ocean. On a blustery day in July, I stood on the deck of her diesel-powered cruiser and looked across the jade green sea to one of the wildest and least known parts of Alaska.

We were following a wind-battered coast, skirting the coves, bays, and inlets that fringe the new Kenai Fjords National Park. Off our starboard bow, clouds skimmed the peaks of the Kenai Mountains on the mainland. Glaciers, splintered by crevasses, glinted in the evening sun, bright streaks on the slopes of dark rock. Along the base of the mountains spruce and hemlock and leafy undergrowth competed for space. A more delicate green brushed the steepest slopes where avalanches had obliterated the evergreens and only alders grew. This coastal strand, so thickly grown, gave some respite from the hard lines of a landscape scarcely disturbed by man.

Populous Anchorage lies only 130 highway miles to the north. But with the stormy gulf on one side and the Harding Icefield dominating its highlands, the park terrain has remained an isolated wilderness—a realm of bears, foxes, wolverines, mountain goats, and moose.

No one lives there permanently, not even the rangers who have their headquarters in nearby Seward. In 1968 a party of mountaineers braved howling winds and treacherous weather to cross the Harding Icefield. It was the first complete crossing on record. The icefield, roughly 35 by 15 miles, lies mostly within the park.

But now the protective isolation is beginning to crumble. "By designating this area a national park, the government is, in effect, saying to the public, 'you will go there,'" said Pam. "Just in the last two years we've begun to see a major increase in tourism."

Perhaps the best way to approach the Kenai Fjords is by boat, for the food-rich waters lapping or lashing at the shore attract a marvelous variety of life—breeding harbor seals and sea lions, whales and bewhiskered sea otters, and some 175,000 seabirds of 18 breeding species. And the coast makes so many twists and turns around cliffs and headlands and slender, verdant spits that the park actually confronts the ocean for 600 magnificent miles.

Glacier-fed cascade thunders down Storm Mountain in Alaska's fjord-creased parkland. Largely inaccessible to humans except by boat or aircraft, the green cliffs, icy interior, and tortuous shore support a varied wildlife realm. The arctic tern summers here, then heads for summer in the Southern Hemisphere. Some fly 25,000 miles yearly, equal to a trip around the world—the longest known bird migration.

ABOVE: WAYNE LANKINEN/DRK PHOTO
OPPOSITE: STEVEN C. KAUFMAN

Photographs by George Herben

49

Towering above this coastal strip and rimming half the horizon, the jagged Kenai Mountains rise some 6,000 feet; they deflect the storm clouds that roll in from the North Pacific and trap the moisture, chilling and condensing it to produce snowfalls that can exceed 400 inches a year. Over thousands of years the accumulation of snow and ice created the Harding Icefield, entombing hundreds of square miles of the Kenai Mountains. Occasionally a high peak, craggy and naked, thrusts up from the featureless plain. Called nunataks, these solitary teeth of rock preside over this empty world, where the shrieking wind only accentuates the silence.

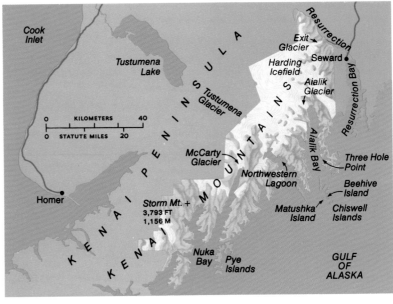

KENAI FJORDS NATIONAL PARK. 669,000 acres. MAJOR FEATURES: Wild coast— fjords, glaciers, forested mountains, Harding Icefield; seabirds, sea mammals. FACILITIES: Park office at Seward; Exit Glacier trail. ACCESS AND ACCOMMODATIONS: Air, local ferry service to Homer, Seward; bus to Seward. Gravel road to park. Air, boat charters. Lodging at Seward, Homer. ACTIVITIES: Sailing, cruising; coastal wildlife watching; icefield hiking; glacier viewing.

FOR INFORMATION: Superintendent, Box 1727, Seward, Alaska 99664.

From these heights glaciers inched down, gouging out the fjords. Many of the glaciers melted long ago, but even now 34 major, named glaciers and uncounted smaller ones spill down. Five bulldoze their way to the sea. The icefield also breeds cold winds that funnel through the valleys, compressing and growing in fury along the way, reaching a hundred miles an hour.

These williwaws churn the water into a white maelstrom of foam and spray. "In winds like that the anchors just don't hold," said Pam, easing back on the throttles of her 43-foot cruiser, *Shaman*, "so I buck the heavy seas and head for home. Some days it's really rough going. Other days, even with the ten-foot tides, it's flat calm.

"It's different each time I go out. One time we had 30 killer whales swimming along with us for three or four miles. The minke whales love to get under the boat to rub their backs, and the porpoises dive and leap around us just for play."

In June, she went on, Steller's sea lions bear pups on smooth rock ledges of the Pye Islands. Females keep the newborn from sliding into the water, where killer whales are waiting, by grabbing them with their mouths and moving them to safety.

As we left Resurrection Bay and turned toward Aialik Bay, we watched a pod of sea otters floating on their backs, front paws clasped to their chests, totally at ease on the heaving surface. Pam idled the engines at Three Hole Point, where pounding surf had sculptured a steep islet into a series of arches. The islands that jut up all along the coast—most lying just outside park boundaries—are fragments of mountains sinking into the sea. Sometimes several feet drown at once—as happened during the awful earthquake of 1964.

Near Aialik Glacier, with its great white length curving out of sight into the clouds, the landscape was all rock and ice and dolorous wind. Just off the mouth of Aialik Bay are the Chiswell Islands, home to nearly two-thirds of all the nesting seabirds on the peninsula's

Icebound torrent of Exit Glacier melts into a meandering stream near Seward. A new path lures park visitors to touch the edge of the glacier, one of countless ice streams radiating from Harding Icefield. Exit earned its name as a handy route down from the icefield.

FOLLOWING PAGES: *Aialik Glacier's mile-wide snout dips to the sea, bringing mineral-rich nutrients to the food web of Kenai's waters.*

spectacular south coast. The islands are actually part of the Alaska Maritime National Wildlife Refuge, but nonetheless a part of the park experience for seaborne visitors to the fjords.

The islands are so precipitous that boats have almost no place to land. On the other hand, if the islands had nice beaches or coves, they would not be such safe havens. So I was told by Edgar P. Bailey, an adventurous biologist with the U. S. Fish and Wildlife Service.

Ed camped on Matushka Island, one of the Chiswells, in 1976 to survey the rhinoceros auklets and fork-tailed storm-petrels that show up at darkest night, the dusklike summer hours between one and three. Matushka was so steep, he said, "we had to tie our tent to the trees to keep from falling off the cliff. Thousands of storm-petrels flew in and swarmed around the island, filling the darkness with the rustle of wings. From as far as 200 miles at sea, where they feed, the storm-petrels zeroed in on their nests in rock crevices or burrows, even in dense fog. It seems these birds use a sense of smell to help locate their nests, but no one knows for sure how they navigate over the open ocean to find a small island in fog, mist, and rain. Some think they may respond to changes in the earth's magnetic field.

"We were unable to go ashore on Beehive Island, which rises nearly vertically from the sea, but we pulled up beside it and counted

thousands of tufted puffins nesting there. These chunky birds airlift food to their chicks, stacking capelin in their parrotlike beaks so that the fish hang out the sides of their mouths. The birds sometimes get so overloaded they can barely take off from the water."

The other residents of the Chiswells were equally fascinating. Hundreds of common murres, looking like small penguins with wings, lined open rock ledges where the females lay their eggs. Oddly enough, these birds do not build nests, but nature has given their eggs a pear shape, so they do not easily roll away. "Murres," Ed told me, "are the best divers among the seabirds of North America, routinely going down to 200 feet, but with records reaching 350 feet."

CYNTHIA RUSS RAMSAY, NATIONAL GEOGRAPHIC STAFF. OPPOSITE: GEORGE HERBEN

Vestige of the Ice Age, Harding Icefield blankets unnamed peaks in the rugged Kenai Mountains. Protruding summits— nunataks—bear scars of glacial scouring, evidence of the ice mass that once covered them. Some 28,000 square miles of Alaska still lie under ice. Harding visitors ski, hike, and snowshoe. A few—like John Berryman, left, and Glenn Filbert—brave whiteout and storm to try a crossing.

Glaucous-winged gulls seasoned the wind with their shrill cries. I watched a small flock in pursuit of a bald eagle that probably had come too close to their nests. It is hard to believe that bald eagles, surviving precariously in the lower 48 states, had a bounty on them in Alaska as recently as 1953. The authorities there paid up to two dollars for a set of claws in the mistaken belief that eagles reduced the fishermen's salmon harvest. Recent studies show that the birds dine mostly on dead or dying salmon.

From the coast, so abundant with wildlife, I went to the sparkling emptiness of the Harding Icefield—a ten-minute flight from Seward in a chartered ski plane. Beyond the Resurrection River, heavy with silt, we came upon the jumbled face of Exit Glacier, its searing blue depths glimmering from crevasses. Near the head of the glacier the pilot pointed toward creamy white spots against the hard glare of the snow—five mountain goats that were somehow attracted to such a forbidding place.

For Glenn Filbert and John Berryman, University of Alaska students attempting a crossing of the icefield, the lure was adventure. My plane landed in a spray of snow near their dome tent. They had just spent four days marooned in a whiteout, when sky, snow, and ice combine to produce a landscape without contour, horizon, or shadow. "From a little distance it looked like our tent was adrift in a white mist," said Glenn. Finally the sun poked through, spreading a bright orange glow. In the eerie light the surrounding mountains seemed to float above the snow.

Now, as bright sunshine found diamonds in the snow, John and Glenn broke camp and set out on skis. I watched them become specks

At home and abundant in Kenai Fjords, horned puffins, birddom's grave clowns, crown a rocky outcrop. Using their wings for propulsion, they "fly" swiftly underwater in pursuit of fish. Ruddy turnstones flip beach stones and shells in search of insect food. Ruddy coats, like bright faces of the puffins, distinguish birds in breeding season. Some 65 bird species live along the coast.

of color in the encompassing whiteness, and I felt myself shrinking in the dazzling expanse around me.

Curious to learn how they had fared, I telephoned them some days later. The icefield's capricious weather had dealt them one more violent turn. One night a storm swept in, collapsing the tent. "We struggled to dig a snow cave," Glenn told me, "but we kept getting blown off our feet." They scrambled to some shallow crevasses and huddled under an overhang until the storm blew over. Then they zigzagged down Tustumena Glacier's maze of crevasses, chanced upon some boaters at Tustumena Lake, and arranged for a ride out.

In 1982 park rangers blazed a path alongside Exit Glacier and brought the icefield within range of a day's hike, albeit a steep and strenuous one. Nine miles by road from Seward and two miles along a gravel path, Exit Glacier is the only place where visitors can see the park without chartering a plane or boarding a boat. Here the immense, unhurried power of a glacier looms only an arm's length away. I walked along its terminus, where melting crevasses had split the ice into gleaming columns, menacing but wonderfully blue. I could see rocks embedded in the depths and could hear the summer runoff gurgling along under the glacier's base. I crouched in the dripping hollow of a cave that was melting into a massive wall.

Exit Glacier became accessible when a footbridge was completed across the Resurrection River in 1982. Eventually other facilities will allow the public to use and enjoy more of the park. The ultimate challenge, the one the Park Service always faces, will be to strike a balance between use and preservation of the Kenai Fjords wilderness.

Graceful leviathan, a humpback explodes from Aialik Bay, spreading its flipper wings before splashdown. Breaching may send a message, pose a threat, or shake off parasites—its purpose still puzzles scientists. But it seems contagious: One whale starts, others follow.

FOLLOWING PAGES: *Nuka Bay fjordlands seem frozen in time, belying the restless forces that reshape the Kenai coast. Flowing ice quarries and abrades, gouging deep valleys; fingers of the sea reach in to create the breathtaking fjords. Earthquakes bring swifter change: The coastland sank as much as six feet on Good Friday of 1964, and high tide today floods a mine entrance at Nuka Bay.*

DENALI

By Cynthia Russ Ramsay

A SINGLE NARROW ROAD winding through a pristine wilderness leads visitors to one of the greatest spectacles in North America. For 90 miles the road, mostly gravel, saunters across treeless tundra and wooded riverbanks. It meanders up mountain passes and skirts lofty ridges. Every bend may bring memorable sightings of wildlife—sure-footed Dall's sheep dotting a scree slope, grizzly cubs toddling ahead of their watchful mother, or bands of migrating caribou.

Every few miles offers a new vista of the Alaska Range vaulting high above emerald slopes—one extravagant snow-mantled creation after another until finally the towering majesty of Mount McKinley comes into view and dominates the southern sky.

Here in these untrammeled lands, formerly called Mount McKinley National Park, any visitor can immerse himself in the wilderness drama—yet return each night to the comfort of lodges or campgrounds a short bus ride away. This wilderness offers mass transit.

Four hours pass from the time one of the shuttle buses leaves the Riley Creek Information Center until it rumbles to a stop at Eielson Visitor Center, spectacular for viewing McKinley on clear days. It takes another hour to reach Wonder Lake. Along the 90 miles a driver may stop the bus many times—when a red fox trots alongside, when a golden eagle glides into view, or when someone spots grizzlies feeding like cattle on alpine grasses.

Many people are happy to park their cars and let someone else do the driving. "We would have driven right by if the bus driver hadn't stopped to point out the band of caribou moving across the broad graveled valley," admits one enthusiastic passenger. Every now and then someone hops off to head into the backcountry to spend an hour or two—or a week—in the solitude.

No cavalcades of cars block the road. There are fewer traffic noises to drown the roar of moose or the whistle of a hoary marmot. Private cars may travel only as far as their campground destinations. It has been this way since 1972, when the Park Service limited the use of automobiles and provided transportation. The action anticipated the increase in traffic as the new Anchorage-Fairbanks highway gave motorists easy access to the park. The number of visitors did indeed soar, from 44,000 in 1971 to 320,000 in 1983, making the park, now renamed Denali—the High One, the Athapaskan Indian name for Mount McKinley—Alaska's most popular tourist attraction. "By limiting traffic we're trying to accommodate the summertime crowds,

Ascending the crown of the continent, climbers on fixed lines toil up the West Buttress, a ridge on the most popular route to Mount McKinley's 20,320-foot summit; the trek scales 13,000 feet in 12 miles. Nearby Mount Foraker soars to 17,400 feet. Denali's heights test skilled climbers; most visitors come to look—at the peaks and at the wildlife, including hoary marmots (above) sparring in play.

DENALI NATIONAL PARK AND PRESERVE. 6,028,000 acres. MAJOR FEATURES: Tallest peak in North America; superb wildlife array—grizzlies, wolves, wolverines, lynxes, foxes, moose, caribou, Dall's sheep; varied birdlife. FACILITIES: Campgrounds, hiking trails, visitor centers, park bus. ACCESS AND ACCOMMODATIONS: Auto road and air, rail, and bus service to park; private autos restricted in park. Air taxi to park areas. Lodging, supplies in park and along perimeter road; headquarters at Denali Park. ACTIVITIES: Wildlife watching, mountaineering, backpacking, cross-country skiing, dogsledding, fishing. Sport hunting in preserve. FOR INFORMATION: Superintendent, Box 9, Denali Park, Alaska 99755.

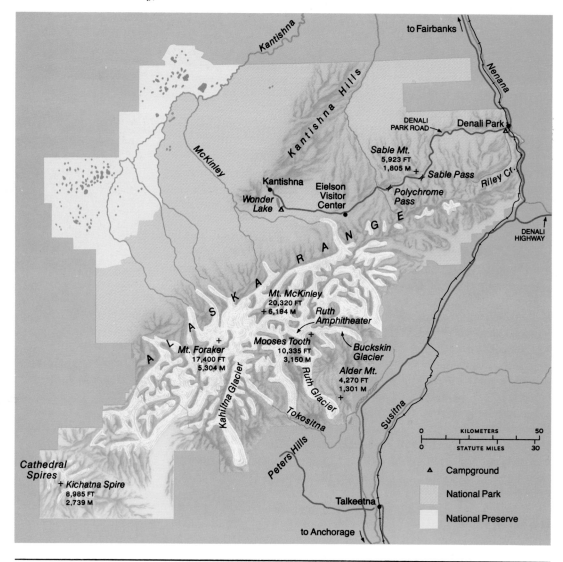

yet retain the elements of wilderness along the park road," says Tom Griffiths, Denali's chief ranger. "In this way, those who come may enjoy glimpses of wildlife wandering as freely as in the early days."

By September, however, snows bring almost instant winter and soon close the road. For nearly eight months of the year the land lies in an icy grip as temperatures plunge below zero, to 40 below or more. It may seem that the park also closes then, but it never does. Visitors trickle in, and among the wild inhabitants only the grizzly, the arctic ground squirrel, and the hoary marmot slumber through the long winter season.

Life goes on for the caribou that paw the snow aside to feed on lichens, for the voles and lemmings, and for the foxes, ermines, and martens that hunt them. Even on the coldest days black-capped chickadees hang upside down on spruce branches, probing the snow-free undersides for dormant insects. Along the rivers, frozen to a glistening pallor, moose sustain themselves on willow twigs, disdaining the dry leaves tinted russet by the frost. Thick fur, fluffed against the cold, insulates the snowshoe hares. They have shed summer brown for inconspicuous white, but the camouflage does not always thwart such hunters as the lynx and the great horned owl.

Fresh tracks in the snow reveal the comings and goings of even the shiest animals. Such tracks have helped Dr. Gordon Haber, an ecologist, to keep tabs on wolf packs and their prey within the park's boundaries. To the wolves his circling Super Cub became so familiar, said Gordon, that "they ignored it as they might a large noisy bird."

He has been most impressed by the elaborate teamwork within the 10-to-15-member wolf packs as they hunt caribou, moose, and Dall's sheep. Sometimes, he said, one or two wolves distract the prey while the rest make a sneak attack. In another common strategy the wolves position themselves around an animal and systematically force it into deep snow or heavy brush where escape is difficult.

"I've also watched them chase prey to places where other wolves are waiting," he continued. "But usually there is no further strategy necessary when they overtake a sheep or caribou. They simply jump on it and eat it. Fifteen wolves can reduce a 200-pound ram to bones in 12 minutes—eating even the blood-soaked snow."

Killing a thousand-pound moose is more difficult. Wolves first size up the prey; most often they retreat without attacking. If the moose is vulnerable—old or weakened, for example—the most experienced hunter in the pack dodges the powerful defensive kicks of the front hooves and tries to bite into the victim's nose. If successful, the lead hunter hangs on by its teeth as the others dash in from the sides and rear, ripping into the soft parts and hind legs.

Grizzlies also go after moose at certain times of year, supplementing their staple diet of roots, grasses, and berries. In spring the bears hunt newborn moose, often succeeding despite a formidable defense by the mothers. In September the rutting season stirs prime bulls to clashes for the right to mate. The bouts are so exhausting that some battlers lie down, hardly able to move. Then a grizzly may feast on bull moose.

In recognition of Denali's unique value for research, a United Nations agency designated it an International Biosphere Reserve in 1974. Nowhere in the subarctic is wildlife so accessible, the interactions in a relatively complete ecosystem so readily visible, the research data so extensive. For many years scientists have been studying wildlife here in all seasons, including the long winters.

Winter is also the time when the rangers at Denali put their sled dogs to work. In the early days they used sleds to patrol against illegal hunting and trapping. Today they fly the winter patrols. But the sledding tradition hangs on; rangers harness the jaunty dog teams to

Waiting time in the mating game: A bull moose patiently attends a cow eating aquatic plants in the Wonder Lake shallows. Bulls lose appetites and forego solitary wandering during the rituals of rutting season. Competing for mates, they threaten rivals by thrashing brush

with their massive antlers. If this fails, they butt head-on. Moose, Dall's sheep, caribou, grizzlies—big animals come frequently into view in a sanctuary relatively easy to reach; more than 300,000 visitors a year tour Denali, arriving by car, bus, train, or air. From campgrounds such as the one at Wonder Lake hikers explore a parkland that tripled in size in 1980.

So steep the snow can't stick to its granite walls, mile-high Mooses Tooth guards the Great Gorge of Ruth Glacier on McKinley's southern flanks. The gorge funnels ice from the mountain-walled Ruth Amphitheater, where air taxis deliver skiers and climbers. A tent site (below) offers solitude and a grand vista of an ice-carved valley in Denali's southeastern corner.

make backcountry rounds, hauling trash and performing chores in areas where summer travel would harm the fragile tundra.

In recent years visitors have also begun to find the park a remarkable place for cross-country skiing and for mushing a trail behind dogs. One of my own memorable winter experiences took place in April, a mile high in the heart of the Alaska Range, which dominates the park and arcs across the lower third of the state for 650 miles.

The snow lashing the taut nylon of our dome tent sounded like staccato blasts of sand. Inside, the frozen condensation of our breaths crusted the walls with rime. Outside, Mount McKinley, soaring almost three miles directly above us, had disappeared into the white void. Nor could we see the sheer granite faces and great snow cornices of the other mountains ringed around us. Just 200 feet away the bamboo wands that marked the crevasse-free landing spot on the glacier seemed to float in an abyss bereft of ground or sky.

"Weather is part of the Alaska experience, and so is patience," said Brian Okonek, a young mountain guide who radiates enthusiasm. "We have no alternative but to hunker down and wait until the plane can come for us." As he spoke he fired up the camp stove to melt snow for water. The April storm held us captive for four days in the Ruth Amphitheater, a spectacular part of the nearly four million acres added to the park in 1980. From the south face of McKinley

three arms of the Ruth Glacier spill down and merge into this mountain-rimmed expanse that seems unconnected to the green earth. Yet just 30 minutes away by plane lies Talkeetna, a small community three hours from Anchorage by car or train. And a five-minute flight from the amphitheater is the Kahiltna Glacier, the staging area for most ascents of McKinley.

Though the mountain walls are extreme, the icy arms of the Ruth are gentle, and skiers are arriving in increasing numbers. On the brilliant day of our arrival we headed toward Mooses Tooth, a gigantic

block of naked rock at the entrance of the Great Gorge of the Ruth. The gorge, wedged between granite cliffs nearly a mile high, forms a funnel for the immense accumulation of ice in the amphitheater. "If you want to humble someone," said Brian, "take him out here."

By evening an elongated lenticular cloud capped McKinley, indicating deteriorating weather. During the stormy days that followed I spent many hours in the tent listening to Brian talk of expeditions on McKinley. In 1983 a record number of 709 men and women set out for the 20,320-foot summit; only 438 made it. The physical challenge, weather, and poor planning all play a part in the failure of climbing expeditions. Obsessed with getting to the top, some climbers push ahead in the face of storm clouds. Storms on McKinley are frequent and vicious. In a recent year one out of five climbers suffered frostbite; seven died of exposure in a single incident in 1967.

Altitude sickness is another hazard. The heights of McKinley have less oxygen than equivalent elevations in the Himalayas. Dr. Peter Hackett, a medical researcher, explains why: "Since the atmospheric layer is thinner at the Poles, climbers just ascend through it faster, encountering oxygen levels found elsewhere at much higher elevations." For two seasons Peter and his colleagues at the University of Alaska High Latitude Research Project examined climbers in a camp laboratory at 14,300 feet; a surprising number suffered from hypertension, dehydration, insomnia, headaches, and nausea. Altitude also dulls the mind. In another McKinley study climbers had more difficulty with the same math problem at 18,000 feet than at sea level.

The Park Service keeps track of everyone on McKinley and nearby Mount Foraker. Climbers must register in Talkeetna, where they are

Sorcery of sun and lowering sky casts twin rainbows and kindles the trunks of paper birch and white spruce. Summer brings many wet days; rain can turn to snow at any time. With late summer the berries ripen; in autumn the blond grizzly (right) may still enjoy a sweet harvest before winter's sleep. Though they can down big prey, grizzlies dine mostly on plants.

FOLLOWING PAGES:
Accustomed to humans in the park, these Dall's sheep rest easy at a hiker's slow approach near Polychrome Pass. The park enforces a "wildlife watcher's code of ethics" to curb harassment of animals.

briefed on potential problems. When a group fails to return on time, the rangers alert air-taxi operators to be on the lookout. The rangers, excellent climbers themselves, direct rescue operations.

The Talkeetna center lies near Denali's huge southern addition, which includes the dramatic Cathedral Spires. These granite pinnacles—about 50 air miles southwest of McKinley—are counted among the ultimate challenges in climbing. Though none rises higher than 8,985-foot Kichatna Spire, their steepness and difficulty force climbers from one hanging belay to another, 3,000 feet straight up from the

ROLLIE OSTERMICK

valley floor. And the threat of foul weather compels climbers to keep going virtually nonstop in the intervals between storms.

I talked with ranger Jonathan Waterman in Talkeetna just after he returned from an exploration of the Cathedral Spires in miserable weather. "On two of the days we had so much snow we were reluctant to move because of avalanche danger. Typically, you wait 24 hours after a storm for the snow to settle," explained Jonathan. The slow pace threatened their planned rendezvous with a plane at Rainy Pass; on the sixth day they went on half rations.

"By day 11 we had come down off the glaciers into the trees, but we were getting hungrier all the time," Jonathan recalled. "One of us tried to spear a ptarmigan with a ski pole. I snuck up on another one and tried to strike it with my pole. But the birds were just too fast." Then the rangers spotted a porcupine and clubbed it. "We skinned it and cooked it with our last packet of soup," said Jon. "When we opened the pot, it didn't smell too good, but it was delicious. The crucial thing was it had a lot of fat for energy." On day 13 they made the rendezvous point, breaking trail in waist-deep snow.

In contrast to the precipitous southern terrain the park's northern addition has the sweep and spaciousness of rolling tundra, scattered

RICK MCINTYRE/ALASKAPHOTO

boreal forest, and marshland and lakes—flatland broken only by the Kantishna Hills. During the stampede of 1905-06 more than 2,000 gold seekers staked nearly every stream in the hills. The rush was short-lived, but small surface yields of placer gold and underground veins of silver and antimony made mining a modest paying proposition through the early '40s. When the price of gold soared in 1972, placer mining came back to the region in a big way. Now about 15 mechanized operations work the gravels in summer.

Two of the miners, Roberta Wilson and Dan Ashbrook, stay on in

Kantishna during the winter—the only permanent residents in the two-million-acre northern addition. "We could winter anywhere, but here we live with Mount McKinley and 200 miles of the Alaska Range shining on the horizon," said Roberta, a vivacious woman with a degree in biochemistry and a fondness for dog mushing. "And the nights are magical with the aurora borealis. A few weeks ago we just lay down in the snow, spellbound as we watched the great streams of yellow-green lights shimmer and flicker across the sky."

Dan and Roberta keep busy trapping lynx, fox, and marten. They had just returned from "wooding" when Richard Stenmark, a Park Service official in Anchorage, and I skied over from the Kantishna airstrip. Dan ushered us into their warm, spacious cabin while Roberta unhitched the dogs. "We cut the trees in the fall, split them once so they don't rot, and let them cure," said Dan. " Then we haul the wood on the sled in winter."

Books lined the cabin walls, a radiotelephone sat on a high shelf, and in a small tub next to the Yukon stove fox and marten pelts were soaking in a tanning solution. Roberta offered slices of carrot cake to tide us over until the moose steak simmered to tenderness. A single moose provides meat through the winter, she said.

Like many miners, Roberta and Dan grumble at the regulations and paperwork the Park Service has imposed on them. "How else can we try to limit the harmful effects of mining on the land?" asked Richard. Washing gravel and sand in placer mining, Richard explained, produces dirty water that must be settled or filtered to keep from silting clear streams. Mining also creates piles of tailings. If they're not recontoured and covered with soil, the tailings leave sterile eyesores. In Kantishna the number of miners who have maintained water quality and reclaimed lands remains very small—though the regulations require all to do so. And the mining roads and tractor trails leave scars on the land that last for decades.

Mining interests lobbied aggressively to keep the Kantishna Hills outside of the park. Conservation groups fought to have the district protected to complete and safeguard a natural ecosystem. As part of a compromise a study was ordered to assess the area's resources. Preliminary reports indicate a significant mineral potential—a condition that may strengthen the arguments of the mining community.

Other problems plague Denali. Conservationists protest that a proposed land exchange would trade away important acreage near the park entrance. Furthermore, a critical 92,000-acre tract of state land was not included in the 1980 additions to the park. All major species in Denali range in and out of this tract; one wolf pack known to have used it for decades has been seriously depleted. Were the wolves trapped or hunted in the critical acreage? But even park boundaries offer no guarantee of protection; one park official says the government would have to maintain a constant air patrol just to begin a successful campaign against poaching.

While Denali's area tripled, tight budgets have kept the staff the same size. Public use continues to increase. The yearly total of visitors has multiplied an astonishing 30-fold since 1962, when naturalists Adolph and Olaus Murie stressed the importance of keeping this unique world forever wild.

In Alaska today, with many more divergent interests placing greater pressures on Denali, that task remains.

A field trip to remember: The big yellow school bus brakes for a grizzly, assuring a safe crossing by the bear and a long look by the passengers. Shuttling along the 90-mile park road, the bus hauls visitors to one of the world's finest wildlife shows. With animals near, riders stay inside; otherwise they may hop off almost anywhere and catch a returning bus hours— or days—later. At summer's ebb the shuttle ends; school bells toll, calling the yellow buses back to their regular jobs.

HELEN RHODE/ALASKAPHOTO. OPPOSITE. BOTH BY RICK MCINTYRE. FOLLOWING PAGES: TOM J. ULRICH

Spires of fireweed edge a woodland still dozing in morning mist near Riley Creek Information Center at the park entrance. Denali's brief growing season begins in June with pasqueflowers (far left) among the early bloomers. Arctic forget-me-nots (left) grow in low mats on the tundra.

FOLLOWING PAGES: Bathed by the northern summer's endless sun, backlighted by the cloud-veiled moon, Mount McKinley floats above Wonder Lake, a wonder to behold.

LAKE CLARK

By Cynthia Russ Ramsay

ALMOST EVERYONE WHO WRITES of the Lake Clark country drops in on Richard Proenneke, landing at his remote lakeshore cabin below the foothills of the Alaska Range. For more than a decade he has inspired those who yearn for a life close to nature in a corner of primitive America. His dedication to the wilderness that beckoned him remains an inspiration, but there is also a lament that Dick has voiced again and again.

"I look at the sharp edges of the mountains in the crisp, clean air," says Dick, "and listen to the creeks pouring water you can drink over the stones. Then I find this junk"—the beer cans, bottles, and cartons he has retrieved from alpine meadows.

An invasion of visitors lured by the aura of a newly created park? Elsewhere, perhaps, but not here. The littering began long before the establishment of Lake Clark National Park and Preserve in 1980. The park area lies a hundred miles southwest of Alaska's metropolis, Anchorage. From the city the white peaks across Cook Inlet hunch along the horizon like a low bank of clouds. Above them rise the volcanic cones of Iliamna and Redoubt—white towers in the southwestern sky. No highway penetrates the mountain barrier, but the Lake Clark region is easily accessible by small plane; its four million acres, wonderfully diverse, have attracted a variety of people for years.

Anglers have come to the famed salmon runs. Hunters have searched forest and tundra for moose and caribou. Commercial clam diggers have spent the summers probing Cook Inlet tidal flats for razor clams, and dozens of fishermen set their nets for salmon, halibut, and herring. A more recent influx has brought backpackers and river runners—boosting the annual total of tourists to more than 15,000.

Dick Proenneke came in 1968 at age 51 to test his resourcefulness in the wilds—and to see if he could enjoy his own company for a year. His published journal indicates how he took to his surroundings: "I never seem to tire . . . of looking down the lake or up at the mountains. . . . If this is the way folks feel inside a church, I can understand why they go." And when I flew in on a frosty September morning, he was still counting each day as a precious experience.

Below their snow-dusted crests the mountains all around us blazed with autumn color as we canoed near the cabin amid the high meadows at Twin Lakes. Blueberry bushes had turned patches of the tundra a glowing burgundy. Leaves of alpine bearberries flamed crimson. Other ground-hugging plants revealed their presence in

Wilderness miniatures: Wild roses mask a stark backdrop of charred woodland; on the tundra a red fox complements September hues. Natural fires add to the park's variety of living things by enriching the soil and clearing the way for new plant succession. For trappers the red fox produces more income than any other furbearer in the parkland.

ABOVE: JIM BRANDENBURG
OPPOSITE: STEPHEN J. KRASEMANN

splotches of yellow, bronze, tan, russet, and chartreuse. Gold shimmered from the balsam poplars on the lower slopes.

Putting in to shore, we started a steep uphill hike on tundra that felt soft and springy underfoot. Fierce winds, severe cold, and brief summers combine to stunt plant life here; not much grows taller than 10 or 12 inches. Lichens flourished everywhere—in a single square yard we found a dozen species. Some looked like diminutive ruffled leaves; some had dainty stalks and spiky branches; others embroidered the rocks with flecks of black, orange, and green. Most common were the tiny, twiggy reindeer lichens; resembling miniature

LAKE CLARK NATIONAL PARK AND PRESERVE. 4,045,000 acres. MAJOR FEATURES: Smoking volcanoes, mountain fastness, glaciers, scenic lakes, wild rivers, wild coast, varied wildlife. FACILITIES: Ranger station at Port Alsworth; hiking routes. ACCESS AND ACCOMMODATIONS: Air charter and taxi from Anchorage, other nearby towns to park; air service to Iliamna. Private lodgings and boat and fishing rentals in park. Supplies at Nondalton, Iliamna. ACTIVITIES: Backpacking, fishing, boating and river running, mountain climbing, wildlife watching. Sport hunting in preserve. FOR INFORMATION: Superintendent, Box 61, 701 C Street, Anchorage, Alaska 99513.

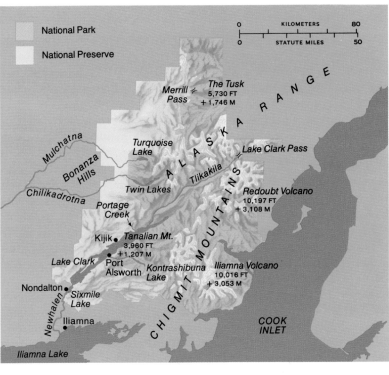

staghorns, they added touches of white to the tapestry of color. Higher up we took in a view of both twins that form Twin Lakes. They were not identical. The upper lake was a raucous turquoise that stunned the eye; the lower, with less glacial silt suspended in its waters, was a deep blue. The lakes are the source of the Chilikadrotna, a foaming river that challenges more and more rafters each year. The Chilikadrotna rushes into the tamer Mulchatna on its westward course to Bristol Bay—the world's richest sockeye salmon fishery. Both rivers swarm with salmon in July.

We paused at a bear den. Since September seemed too early for it to be inhabited, I was persuaded to crawl inside. I fitted comfortably into the tidy burrow, but it would have little room to spare for the rotund black bear we observed through binoculars the next day. I watched its head swing from side to side and bob up and down as it fed virtually nonstop on berries, stripping the leaves and fruit with its long tongue. In contrast, the big-antlered moose following a cow showed no interest in food. Indeed, bulls are so aroused during the rut that they eat very little from mid-September to mid-October. With no place to hide on the wide-open tundra, we had to view the animals from a considerable distance, or they would bolt. We kept very still and hoped the wind would not carry our scent to frighten the shy creatures. Dick noted an exception. The caribou "are so curious," he said jokingly, "that you could shoot one a dozen times before it leaves because it will come closer and circle you for a better look." He was exaggerating, of course, and there was no way anyone could make him test his assertion. He gave up hunting years ago.

In winter Dick's only near neighbors are the red squirrels and impudent gray jays, greedy for his sourdough pancakes. But Dick is just one of 50 permanent residents of the parkland; they include former Alaska governor Jay Hammond and operators of several fishing lodges. Most live along the green waters of Lake Clark, which stretches some 40 miles beside the beauty of the Chigmit Mountains.

With the Chigmits the Aleutian Range begins its grand arc to the southwest and out to sea. The Chigmits have not yet acquired the celebrity they deserve, and the name did not prepare me for the panorama of serried crags, glaciers, lakes, and gorges that seemed some artist's inspired vision of the Alps.

Two low passes provide access into this domain, and on clear summer days it is not unusual for 60 planes a day to fly through for landings on mirror lakes and gravel bars in the park. On one of those mornings I landed near Lake Clark Pass to join rangers Tom Betts and Tim Wingate on a hunting patrol—45 miles down the Tlikakila River by raft to where the icy stream emptied into Little Lake Clark.

On the lookout for poachers, Tom and Tim would keep track of planes flying overhead and scan the gravel bars for recent tire marks. Planes with balloon tundra tires can land almost anywhere, noted Tom, adding that a good Super Cub pilot can put his plane down on a strip no more than 150 feet long.

Portaging half a mile to where the flow of the Tlikakila could buoy the raft, we passed a rusting 55-gallon fuel drum— one of the "tundra flowers" cached by aviators that mark man's passage across Alaska's wilderness. On the gravel bars the sedges, emblazoned by frost, cast a red haze. The cottony seed heads of fireweed quivered with every sharp breeze, and when they broke loose the white tufts created flurries close to the ground.

After we left the pass area, massive slopes crowded the river. Their upper flanks have such steep pitches that avalanches had swept chutes bare of vegetation. Every turn of the river brought us new vistas—snowcapped mountains, shining glaciers, rippling cascades. Tim took a special delight in the fact that the mountains had no names: "It makes them seem unused and untouched."

The frenzied wheeling and diving of bald eagles, ravens, and gulls detoured us to a side stream to see what was going on. Salmon—more than 30 sockeyes with tails thrashing—were digging redds, where the females would lay their eggs. Incredibly, the salmon had found their way from Bristol Bay, up the Kvichak River to Iliamna Lake, then up the Newhalen River to Sixmile Lake, across Lake Clark, up the Tlikakila, and finally to this sliver of a spring-fed stream.

At the site of our planned pickup by a motorboat, a brown bear was patrolling the beach. Somewhat reluctantly, or so it seemed, the bear lumbered off as we approached. Nearby, Tom found the carcass of a

In a pristine reflection of the park's dual appeal, 6,000-foot peaks tower above Turquoise Lake in the western region. The lake's low peninsula provides a campsite with a view, and the tundra foothills offer prime

terrain for backpackers—as well as forage and calving grounds for some of the 20,000 caribou in the Mulchatna herd. From the Lake Clark region the Alaska Range runs north to the interior, and the Chigmit Mountains and the Aleutians sweep southwest down the Alaska Peninsula.

moose. The bear would certainly be back to claim this prize, and nothing could be worse than to be in its way—which is exactly where we would be if we waited for the boat. So it was with renewed vigor that Tom and Tim rowed the extra four miles to a lodge.

The rest of my stay was spent along the shores of Lake Clark. Glen Alsworth, bush pilot and pastor of Port Alsworth's Bible Church, knows no other home. For him Lake Clark is a sanctuary. Nearly all of the 30 tightly knit members of the Port Alsworth settlement are there at the invitation of Glen's father, Babe, a legendary bush pilot who homesteaded 160 acres along the lake in the 1940s.

"Dad could have sold land to some people for a lot of money," Glen told me. "Instead he leased it for nothing to people who shared his old-fashioned morality and values and wanted a Christian atmosphere in which to raise their kids. We wouldn't trade the peace and joy the Lord has given us for any material wealth."

A short, blond man of 29, with a face that seems incapable of a scowl, Glen had just endured a tragedy. The nephew he helped raise had died in a plane flipped by a sudden gust during takeoff. "Few places rival this area for turbulence and tricky winds," said Glen. "The wind builds through Lake Clark Pass and strikes the mountains

STEPHEN J. KRASEMANN

at this end of the lake. Then it burbles over them, blowing in all directions. In places winds drop out of the sky like bombs—creating whirling waterspouts where they hit the lake."

The park staffs a field headquarters at Port Alsworth. In the early years of the park's existence rangers spent much time building friendship and understanding. The effort seems to be paying off.

"As time goes on more and more Alaskans are recognizing the need for regulations to protect the land from the wear and tear of too many people," said Sharon Van Valin, owner of a luxurious lodge on the lake. "For years we lived in total freedom. It's one of the reasons we came here. Now with the crowds that have come in the last three years, we find ourselves asking for controls." Roger Contor, newly appointed director of the Park Service's Alaska Regional Office, described the management techniques. For a time, he said, rangers were just dealing with problems that might leave permanent damage. The ban on all-terrain vehicles—they can scar the landscape for years—was strictly enforced. But sportsmen who fished without a license were at first given polite warnings instead of tickets.

It will take time and money, Roger said, to build a staff adequate to manage the park as the law intends. "But time is on our side," he maintained. "We have the boundaries; we have the real estate."

Others see problems ahead. For example, when Natives receive title to the ancestral lands they seek under current law, a substantial chunk of the coast will be removed from the park. The shoreline of Lake Clark itself is also marked with homesteads and with allotments to Tanaina Indians from the village of Nondalton. Once the land is in private hands, the owners can do as they please. Jack Hession, Alaska representative of the Sierra Club, worries about plans for subdivisions within the parkland. Will vacation homes be next? Park Service officials say they're looking into the possibility of buying up the lands, trading for them, or acquiring scenic easements. But there are no easy answers—nor inexpensive ones.

Paul and Agnes Cusma, an Indian couple, have not yet received title to their allotment, but they regularly go to their cabin on Lake Clark—a 30-mile trip by skiff from Nondalton. When I met them they had come with a pressure cooker—so Agnes could put up berries—and a CB radio. They also fished for salmon, which Agnes dips in brine and cures in the smokehouse. A mainstay of the Indian diet, the chewy strips were a delicacy to me. After freeze-up and "snow-go" time, the Cusmas would come up to the cabin by snow machine to jig for whitefish, grayling, and lake trout through holes in the ice.

In my journeyings around Lake Clark I traveled by motorboat and plane. No one who has ever seen the alder thickets clogging the shores and lower slopes would suggest walking. It takes an elevation of 1,800 feet to leave the brush behind. A few trails exist. One leads from Port Alsworth to Kontrashibuna Lake. Another—a marshy route—leads to the abandoned Indian village of Kijik.

A lovely path leads from Tish and Howard Bowman's place on Lake Clark to their placer mine on Portage Creek. Stands of cranberry and blueberry bushes along the trail slowed our pace as Tish and I sampled their delicate sweetness. Scraggly black spruce rose in dark columns all around us. "Bottle-brush trees" they're called, and one look at their blunt tops tells you why. I find them strangely appealing. For me these spindly sentinels symbolize all the resilient forms of life that survive in the hardscrabble world of Alaska.

A little way up a slope Tish and I found Howard panning for "color" in Portage Creek. "Listening to the water ouzels and fishing for trout are the real rewards," said Howard, an employee of the Federal Aviation Administration in Iliamna. "The trail up here is not just a trail, for it has moose tracks on it. The mountains are grander because grizzlies are living there. And the sense of space and peace are worth more than I can say. The real gold up here is the way of life."

I knew Howard was right, for I have indeed come away from Lake Clark feeling richer. And if the future doesn't vandalize the wealth of beauty and wildlife, the real gold will be there for others to enjoy.

Eager fishermen cast from plane floats before taking off from Port Alsworth on the south shore of Lake Clark—the park's namesake—to fish in nearby rivers and lakes. Arctic char and grayling, Dolly Varden trout, northern pike, and five kinds of salmon lure thousands of fishermen to this "fly-in park" each year. Lodges and private homes fringe a number of the lakes; the area has long served as a retreat for residents of Anchorage and other towns across Cook Inlet.

The panting of huskies and the calls of the musher mark the passage of a sled across Lake Clark. Bob Tracey runs a 60-mile course to check traplines; in place of snowmobiles he prefers traditional transport to pursue the traditional enterprise of fur-trapping, legal in the park.

JIM BRANDENBURG

FOLLOWING PAGES: Along a sharp ridge near Portage Lake, Dall's sheep crop the mountain growth; keen eyes and knowledge of choice grazing spots beyond the reach of predators spell survival for these northern relatives of the bighorns. The white mountain sheep bear the name of the American explorer-naturalist William Healey Dall. A biographer dubbed him "first scientist of Alaska."

Fresh from a glacier, a shallow stream flails the boulders near Turquoise Lake. Like many features in the park, the stream has no name. The Tusk (left), aptly named, rises 5,730 feet near Merrill Pass, one of two air access routes to the western divide. There lie the tundra slopes, the long lakes, and the web of waters linked to the great Bristol Bay commercial salmon fishery.

FOLLOWING PAGES: Chigmit spires pierce a sunrise sky above the spruce-hung shores of Lake Clark. On this September day the sun goes higher; in winter it does not top the peaks for months.

MARK MCDERMOTT/ALASKAPHOTO. OPPOSITE: STEPHEN J. KRASEMANN. FOLLOWING PAGES: JIM BRANDENBURG

KATMAI

By Cynthia Russ Ramsay

THE AIR WAS ALIVE with the raucous chatter of magpies, and in the foaming rush of the Brooks River silvery salmon were hurling themselves up the waterfall on their way to their spawning streams.

Then it happened. A dark, shaggy form of massive proportions shuffled out from the foliage along the far bank and reared up, sniffing the air with its quivering nose. Unperturbed by our human scent, the bear flopped heavily into the water where it pounced on the thrashing fish until finally it seized one with its frightening claws.

I knew that with one swat of its paws a bear can kill a man. It can bend a bar of steel. And in galloping pursuit it can speed up to 40 miles an hour. Yet, with only a little nervous hesitation, I had followed a park ranger to this place half a mile from Brooks Camp lodge and found myself not 40 yards from a 700-pound Alaska brown bear. Astonishing! But this was August in Katmai National Park and Preserve, and the bears feasting on salmon were accustomed to the steady trickle of human visitors—35 to 60 a day. The hungry bear paid little heed to the enthralled group standing so improbably close in the observation area beside Brooks Falls.

It was dusk. Along the shores of Lake Brooks, half a mile upstream from the falls, bald eagles sat atop the tallest snags; only their white heads, swiveling slowly from side to side, were clearly visible in the pewter light. Elsewhere in Katmai hump-shouldered moose browsed on willows at water's edge, their huge antlers bobbing as they snapped their jaws upward to clip the tender twigs. On the vast sweep of tundra varying hares, voles, and ground squirrels were fleeing red foxes, lynxes, and wolverines—their small scurrying drowned in the hum of swarms of mosquitoes.

Other animals—wolves, beavers, river otters, hawks, falcons, and owls—abound in the four million acres of wild land at the base of the Alaska Peninsula. Katmai's hundreds of miles of swift, crystal streams, fed by snowmelt from the Aleutian Range, form a watershed for one of the most productive sockeye salmon spawning grounds in the world. Beginning in August the streams run scarlet with more than a million salmon making their way up from Bristol Bay in a frenzy to reproduce and then to die. In the same shallow waters live trophy-size rainbow trout, 12-pounders that quicken the hearts of fly-fishermen. The toughest fighters for their size, these beautiful, elusive fish represent the ultimate challenge for anglers.

The variety of wildlife and the extraordinary concentration of

Yearling brown bears feast on salmon near the Brooks Camp visitor complex. Nourished by plentiful food, brown bears of the coastal regions outgrow their kin of the interior, the grizzlies. Largest meat eaters among North American land animals, brown bears may weigh more than 1,500 pounds. Observing them—and hooking such beauties as the 3-pound rainbow trout above—rank high as Katmai attractions.

ABOVE: ROLLIE OSTERMICK
OPPOSITE: STEPHEN J. KRASEMANN

97

KATMAI NATIONAL PARK AND PRESERVE. 4,093,000 acres. MAJOR FEATURES: Volcanic landscape, wild waters, rich salmon, brown bear habitat. FACILITIES: Campground, hiking trails, ranger station at Brooks Camp, van tours to Valley of Ten Thousand Smokes. ACCESS AND ACCOMMODATIONS: Air, boat service to park facilities; dirt road from King Salmon to park edge. Lodging, limited supplies, equipment rentals in park. ACTIVITIES: Bear observation area, birding, backpacking, fishing; river, lake touring. Sport hunting in preserve. FOR INFORMATION: Superintendent, Box 7, King Salmon, Alaska 99613.

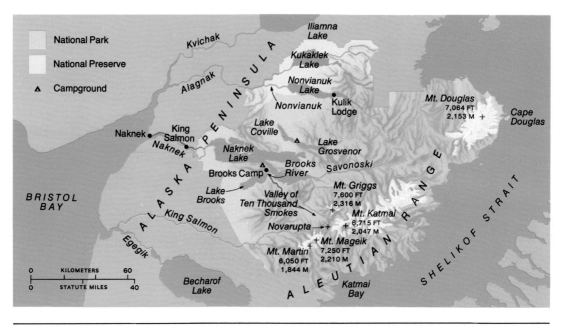

brown bears so readily sighted make a trip to Katmai a unique experience. But there is more—the eerie, pastel wasteland produced by one of the most stupendous volcanic eruptions in recorded history. Dr. Robert F. Griggs, leader of six scientific expeditions to Katmai after the 1912 cataclysm, told of such marvels as ash slides more than a thousand feet high, a boiling crater lake with wisps of steam curling everywhere from its surface, and misty waterfalls cascading into a desert canyon covered with many-colored muds.

Griggs also wrote of a valley "full of hundreds, no thousands—literally, tens of thousands—of smokes curling up from its fissured floor." Prompted by such reports, President Woodrow Wilson in 1918 proclaimed Katmai and its Valley of Ten Thousand Smokes a national monument. Since then the boundaries have been extended four times largely to protect wildlife. Now a 3,669,000-acre park and 424,000-acre preserve, Katmai has become the largest sanctuary for the Alaska brown bear and includes the vital headwaters of the salmon-spawning streams of the Naknek River system.

Today the inferno on the valley floor has cooled. But several of the 12 volcanoes in the park puff steam and ash from time to time, hinting of unbanked fires below the earth's surface. They are part of the immense arc of volcanoes along the Pacific rim—the Ring of Fire.

Katmai, the entire Alaska Peninsula, and the parks of Lake Clark and Kenai Fjords lie astride this unstable zone. Along the arc the great, slowly shifting slabs of earth's crust, called plates, do more than collide; in Alaska the Pacific plate actually plows underneath the North American plate, thrusting up volcanoes from the rock melted by the tremendous heat of the process.

The snowy symmetry of the volcanic cones and the sharp icy jumble of the Aleutian peaks bisect Katmai, raising a formidable barrier between the lake district to the west and the eastern coast. Along this coast the mountains fall sharply to the squally Shelikof Strait, carving a scenic shoreline of fjords, deep bays, gnarled headlands, and steep pebbly beaches awash with squishy kelp. Isolated by the spine of mountains, the rarely visited coast has been left to the bears, marine mammals, and seabirds.

Like most visitors, I flew to Brooks Camp, landing on Naknek Lake in a floatplane that connected with the daily jet from Anchorage to King Salmon. "For your safety I need to tell you about bears," said ranger Greg Moss, as he greeted the passengers. "Bears have the right-of-way at Katmai, so don't block their path. The bear just wants the trail to keep going. If you should suddenly come upon a bear, clap your hands to get its attention; speak in a calm voice—I always say 'Hey bear.' Then back away slowly. Do not run. It seems to remind bears of prey and triggers a predator response. Besides you can't outrun bears. You also do not turn your back on them because if they know you're scared, they may charge."

The briefing is part of a program to reduce the potential for conflict. "We're trying to keep the bears from learning to associate humans with food," Superintendent Dave Morris told me as we talked at the ranger station near the lodge. "We fly or barge out every piece of garbage produced here and ask visitors at the campground to store their food in a cache we've built on tall stilts. We distribute plastic bags to all fishermen and urge them to wrap their catch immediately and place it in a special fish-cleaning building.

"Bears are basically shy of humans. But they are intelligent, and some have learned that if they approach a fisherman he will drop his fish. Who can blame the bears for pursuing an easy meal?" Especially, Dave added, during July and early August, when the fish in the water are still lively and harder for bears to catch. Later, as the salmon turn red and spawn in the shallows, they are easy prey. Most people cooperate, said Dave, but he has seen men duel bears with their fishing rods. He once saw someone tossing firecrackers at a bear.

The Park Service sometimes finds it necessary to educate younger bears to stay out of the lodge area and campground. "We pepper their backsides with fine pellet birdshot," said Dave. "But we never 'counsel' the bears on the river. The rest of Katmai is their turf." Amazingly, only one person has been hurt by a Katmai bear. The victim had spilled food grease on his jeans and slept in them on a bear trail. A bear bit the grease spot. The man screamed and the bear ran off.

"Brown bears around Brooks Camp are just more tolerant of humans than grizzlies," said Greg Moss on a walk along the riverbank, an excellent place to spot bears. Scientists today regard the Alaska brown bear and the grizzly as races, or subspecies, of the same species—Ursus arctos. "The brown bear," Greg explained, "lives within 200 miles of the coast and can satisfy its huge hunger on the enormous numbers of dying salmon. In the interior the grizzly grazes on the scantier rations of the tundra. The easy abundance has bred a bear larger in size and generally less truculent and less unpredictable than the hard-pressed animal in the interior."

Before we saw them, we heard the sound—an awful, high-pitched bawling. When we rounded a bend, Greg hushed me to silence and pointed across the river, little more than a stone's throw away. Two cubs—one brown, the other honey—were tussling over a piece of fish. Soon the ever watchful mother strode into view and swatted her squabbling offspring on their rumps. Just then another bear emerged soundlessly from the brush a hundred yards downstream. Instantly mother scampered away, herding her cubs before her.

"Bears are solitary creatures. When two bears meet, the less dominant one will run off. A sow is especially wary of old boars, which sometimes kill the cubs," continued Greg. "They're such individuals—one may be scared of his shadow, and the other seems mad at the world. Most of them, even the older ones, play for hours. In the spring I've watched them slide down snow slopes on their backsides. The cubs play even more, wrestling, boxing, and jumping up and down on their mother's back. Bears are even funny to watch sleeping. Sometimes they'll stretch out on their backs with four legs sticking up in the air. In the fall the bears around here get so fat they can't lie down without first digging out a belly bed for themselves."

The bountiful Brooks River, a little stream just over a mile long, has sustained more than well-fed bears. For 4,500 years people had lived near the waters teeming with salmon. "We estimate there are 600 to 800 dwellings in the area, making Brooks River one of the largest archaeological sites in Alaska. Almost every depression in the terrain represents a house site," said Park Service archaeologist Harvey Shields. Over the years archaeologists have unearthed animal bones indicating that people also ate bear, caribou, and porcupine. Artifacts such as potsherds, spear points, and fishing spears also provide glimpses into the daily life of the residents.

"No spears for us. We used gill nets to catch our salmon," said 72-year-old Trefan Angasan, an Aleut who remembers when the Brooks River area was a fish camp for his aunt. Under a Native allotment act she filed for the land in 1971. And according to a determination by the Bureau of Land Management in March 1983, the 120 acres around the river—where the park's major facilities are located—belong to Trefan Angasan, sole heir to his aunt's estate. The Park Service immediately appealed the BLM decision, and the issue was put on hold pending a final resolution. In the meantime Angasan and his relatives regarded the visitors to Brooks Camp as trespassers.

Bears and people go where the salmon are—and so do the rainbows, graylings, and Dolly Vardens. These lively game fish follow the salmon up their spawning streams to feed on the salmon fry as they emerge from the eggs. To the same sparkling waters and nearby lakes come a fraternity of anglers who find no more magic a time than when they are fighting a fish.

Fly-fishermen often find such times on the Alagnak, one of the fabled trout streams flowing through the northern reaches of Katmai. There one day William M. Brumley, Jr., a Texas oilman, stood shin-deep in the water, deftly flicking his line in long, graceful loops.

He was enjoying one of those vacations for which sportsmen pay

One that got away! A sockeye salmon struggling upstream to spawn takes to the air at Brooks Falls. Beyond, a brown bear ignores the flash of silver; more will come. Over a million salmon a year spawn in the waters of Katmai. Might means right in the bears' choice of fishing sites—the best ones go first to the biggest and scrappiest fishers.

JOHNNY JOHNSON

*S*team puffs from the watery crater of Mount Martin, one of a dozen
volcanoes in the parkland. Two of them, Novarupta and Katmai,
erupted in 1912, ejecting a dozen times as much rock, ash, and dust as

Mount St. Helens did in 1980. In addition to the peak named for George C. Martin—first scientist dispatched to the fiery scene in 1912—Mageik, Trident, and Griggs fume intermittently, constant reminders of the seething underground forces that could change the face of Katmai overnight.

Slicing into 45 feet of volcanic debris, Knife Creek drains the cracked slopes in the Valley of Ten Thousand Smokes. When Dr. Robert F. Griggs discovered it, fumaroles filled the valley. He likened it to "all the steam-engines in the world . . . letting off surplus steam in concert."

hundreds of dollars a day to sample streams accessible only by air. Every morning Brumley and the other 15 guests left the comfort of Kulik Lodge and flew off from Nonvianuk Lake. I flew to Kulik from Brooks Camp and joined him on a day's outing. He was the first to land a big one, a 22-inch rainbow, but he had to play it for a while, letting out line for the fish to run, twist and turn, and vault into the air. When, for a moment, the line grew slack, he pulled the trout in, its rose bands and dark iridescent speckles gleaming wetly in the sun.

Wearing waders, I slogged along as Brumley located another spot, then watched him tie a black sculpin on his line. The wet fly was designed to match the rainbow's natural prey that time of year. "These big ol' flies we're using are hard to cast. It's like throwing a string with a rock at the end of it," he said.

"When you get on a river," he added as he chewed on a cigar, "everything else goes out of your mind; it's almost like meditation. But you know, we don't come to catch fish. We come to go fishing." He cast again and again, drawing lovely fluid lines in the air that seemed to encircle him and put him beyond the bounds of conversation.

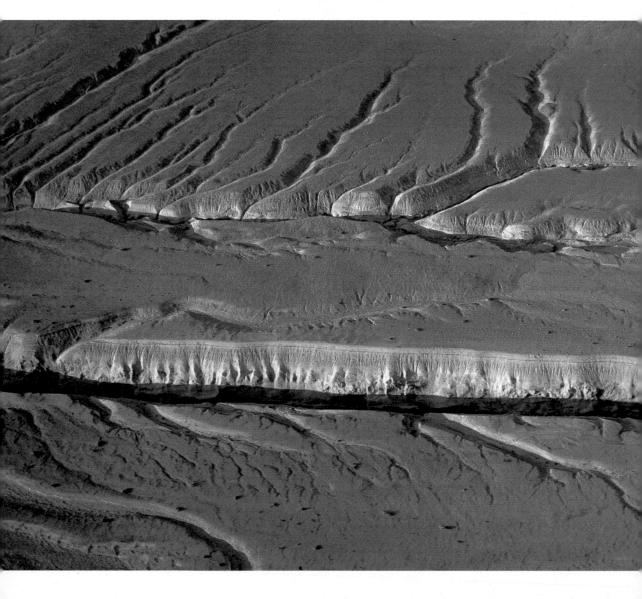

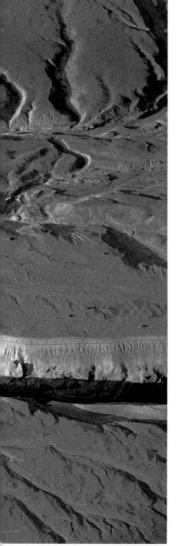

In a silence mellowed by the sweet gurgle of the river, I gazed at the expanse of tundra rolling eastward to the ramparts of the Aleutians. No trees impeded the view even though the elevation did not exceed a thousand feet. The high winds discourage trees, and the landscape, made of such miniatures as mosses and lichens, willow, dwarf birch, and other stunted shrubs, and diminutive flowers, lay open and exposed under a deep and distant sky.

A good 30- or 40-knot wind, I discovered, is part of the Katmai experience. Winds in the Valley of Ten Thousand Smokes can be so fierce that ash and cobbles of pumice whirl through the air in storms that rake hikers, choke the valley, and smother the sky.

There is no way to outwit either Katmai's winds and severe weather or the white sox—a white-legged blackfly many victims consider even more unpleasant than the infamous Alaska mosquito. The bite of this pest may inject both an anesthetic and an anticoagulant. Even though you don't feel them as they attack along the hairline, on the back of the neck, or under trousers on your legs, the welts ooze blood and the itching lasts for days.

Nothing, however, marred the unusual mild and sunny day when I jounced along Nonvianuk Lake in an aluminum skiff with fishing guide Don Swanson. Schools of sockeye salmon, tomato red and almost ready to spawn, hung motionless at the mouths of nameless little creeks awaiting the final changes in their bodies that would send them upstream to dig their spawning nests, or redds, in the gravel. They scattered as we approached, churning the water to a froth.

At the far end of the lake we turned into the Nonvianuk River, which leads to the Alagnak River. Not only are fly-fishermen attracted to the Alagnak, but it is also a prime habitat for bald eagles, and in the last few years it has become increasingly popular for float-fishing trips. By 1982 some 15 commercial operators had started running rafts down the Alagnak for sportsmen who enjoy a little white water as they fish. It became part of the National Wild and Scenic River System with passage of the Alaska Lands Act of 1980.

Backpacking in Katmai has also increased but the numbers are not overwhelming—from 24 in 1970, to 394 in 1983. The scenic spectacle of the Valley of Ten Thousand Smokes remained little visited until 1963, when the Park Service bulldozed a 23-mile road from Brooks Camp to a knoll above the valley. It is still the only road in the park.

I traveled the road with Dr. Terry E. C. Keith of the U. S. Geological Survey. She was studying the chemistry and mineralogy of the deposits that in 1912 buried the valley to depths of 700 feet and more. Terry had much to say about the 60-hour cataclysm. From Novarupta volcano columns of ash shot thousands of feet into the air; a gas-charged avalanche poured down the 15-mile length of the valley. Nothing survived. For years the valley was filled with columns of steam—the ten thousand smokes. As the volcanic deposit cooled, the smokes died out, leaving a dramatic desert of ash congealed into soft, crumbly stone in muted shades of pink, yellow, orange, and beige. Rains, swollen rivers, ice, and winds shaped the crevices and cracks in the cooling crust into gorges, fluted cliffs, and soaring buttresses.

My eyes strayed from the landscape, at once utterly desolate and utterly inspiring, to the awed visitors around me. Never had we seen anything like it. Never would we see its like again. In the great silence the valley spoke to each of us in a clear and eloquent voice.

Rack of moose antlers reaches toward the clouds nudging Baked Mountain, which overlooks the Valley of Ten Thousand Smokes. Alaska boasts the world's largest moose—and moose antlers—and Katmai offers ideal habitat. In winter moose feed on dwarf birch and lowland willow. Come spring, they drift toward higher browse. Pumice-strewn slopes, though, support few plants. Geologists found this rack near Katmai's Savonoski River and flew it here—to add a touch of atmosphere to a hut set up for the University of Alaska's Geophysical Institute.

ANIAKCHAK

By James A. Sugar

WHEN WE AWAKEN for our second morning on the river, the storm is more than 15 hours old. Wind drives the rain into horizontal sheets, saturating my tent. Water puddles around my sleeping bag. Although some of the swiftest rapids of the Aniakchak River rage only a few yards away, the wind and rain drown out the noise of the churning stream.

The wind also triggers small rockslides from the 2,000-foot-high walls that surround us. We camped here only as a last resort. The Aniakchak slowed us down, burned us out. Failing energy and the fear of exposure forced a halt at this vulnerable spot.

In addition to my wife, Jan, and me our rafting party includes park rangers Marc Matsil and Paul Ewers and two professional guides, Stacy Studebaker and Bud Rice. We have extensive outdoors experience but little information to guide us here. We know of only two other attempts to float the river. During one of them the rapids destroyed a raft, and a rafter had to be helicoptered out.

Severe weather and the remoteness of the region are the essence of the Aniakchak River and the 30-square-mile volcanic caldera from which it flows—heart of Aniakchak National Monument and Preserve. It lies in the center of the 500-mile-long Alaska Peninsula, where 15 volcanoes are known to have erupted in the past two centuries. Many more volcanic peaks rise in the Aleutian Islands beyond the peninsula—like the spine and tailbones of some monstrous reptile stretching more than 2,000 miles into the sea.

Local lore abounds with stories of Aniakchak's difficulties. A week earlier at King Salmon, 130 miles away, as we packed our gear into the 1946 Grumman Goose amphibian that was to fly us here, an old-timer asked about our destination. "Takin' them inside Aniakchak crater," pilot Orin Seybert replied. "Who's going?" the old man asked again. "I am," I said.

The questioner hesitated for a few moments, shifted the stub of a well-chewed cigar from one side of his mouth to the other and continued: "Well, I've got a bit of advice for you, boy. If you don't need a psychiatrist going in, you're gonna need one coming out. The last guy who went in there ended up crawling out on his hands and knees all the way to Port Heiden." There is an airstrip with scheduled flight service at Port Heiden, which is near the village of Meshik on the Bering Sea. But between there and the caldera stretch 15 trackless miles of tundra and thickets of alder and willow. A charter flight

Turquoise gem in a stark setting, a small water hole nestles in giant Aniakchak caldera, centerpiece of the new national monument. Born of an explosion 3,500 years ago, the volcano last erupted in 1931. Hardy saxifrage now blooms in the pumice that remains— symbol of rebirth in this once denuded pit.

avoids the rugged hike, but does not guarantee entry into Aniakchak.

As often as not the six-mile-wide caldera looks today as it did in the 1930s to the "Glacier Priest," Father Bernard R. Hubbard: "a huge wash-tub filled with soapsuds running over and down its sides." Masses of cloud and fog are constantly brewing as cold air from the Bering Sea and the warmer air of the North Pacific contend across the Alaska Peninsula and the Aleutians. Intense storms from the western Pacific also sweep across the region. So, while local fliers may pop in during a bit of clear weather, there is no foreseeable hazard of visitor jams at this newly established parkland.

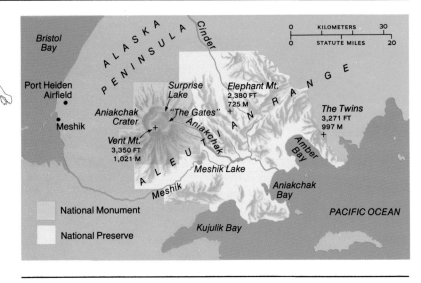

ANIAKCHAK NATIONAL MONUMENT AND PRESERVE. 603,000 acres. MAJOR FEATURES: Volcanic landscape in one of the world's largest calderas. FACILITIES: None. ACCESS AND ACCOMMODATIONS: Air charters at King Salmon, Port Heiden. No lodging or supplies in vicinity of monument. ACTIVITIES: Backpacking, fishing, river running; wildlife watching. Sport hunting in preserve. FOR INFORMATION: Superintendent, Box 7, King Salmon, Alaska 99613.

After loading the Goose with two inflatable rafts and enough backpack and survival gear to last two weeks, our team took off for the 90-minute flight to Aniakchak. We, too, found soapsuds frothing around the caldera, but it was a gorgeous day by Aniakchak standards. Orin, a veteran pilot who started his own flying service at the age of 19, had no trouble descending inside the walls.

Immediately I picked out Surprise Lake, the source of the river, and traced the river's course to the Gates, a narrow opening in the walls. Without this V-shaped gash, warm-water springs feeding the lake would soon have filled the huge bowl, creating a crater lake. With the water draining out, scientists have been able to study the caldera, documenting a score of events—lava flows and formation of cinder cones—that have occurred in the past 3,500 years.

The morning after landing we decided to climb Vent Mountain, a volcano within a volcano, 3,350 feet high and five miles in circumference. Hiking the four miles across the undulating ash fields to the base of the mountain proved easy. Along the way we passed a circular hole several hundred feet deep and filled with water—whose color matched exactly the bright turquoise of Stacy's Navajo ring. On the west side of the caldera we discovered a natural amphitheater composed of alternating bands of red and brown sedimentary rock overlaid with volcanic rock.

Stacy, our botanist, was delightfully surprised at the rich variety of plant life in this hostile climate: fields of lush sedge, mare's tail, and marsh marigold near the lakeshore; orchids crowding the warm springs; tiny, flat cushions and rosettes clinging to life on the windswept ash terraces above the lake oasis.

Once we reached the mountain, the going became much more difficult. The two-hour ascent was like climbing a 40-degree slope covered with ball bearings. The entire mountainside was scree. Near the top each step required caution as the ground gave way underfoot. It was tiring and slow going. It was also dangerous for anyone below. The lead hikers loosened rocks, starting rockfalls. Nearing the summit Marc kicked free a melon-size rock that headed straight for me.

Volcano within a volcano, Vent Mountain (right center) rises from the 30-square-mile caldera. Fed by Surprise Lake, the Aniakchak River flows through a gash in the wall called the Gates. High temperatures on the lunarlike surface indicate potential for more volcanic activity; Mount Veniaminof, 65 miles away, spewed molten rock in 1983.

FOLLOWING PAGES: From Vent Mountain's 3,350-foot summit, hikers gaze out on snow and scree; behind them rises Black Nose, second highest peak on the crater rim.

RIGHT: M. WOODBRIDGE WILLIAMS, NATIONAL PARK SERVICE

FOLLOWING PAGES: STACY STUDEBAKER

At the last moment the rock zigged and I zagged, barely avoiding it.

From the summit we gazed down the 400-foot cliff walls to the cold floor of Vent's crater. Looking out, we could see three other cinder cones inside the huge caldera, which last erupted in 1931. On May 1 of that year, ash and steam shot up from Aniakchak into an incandescent mushroom cloud 20,000 feet high. Eruptions continued for days, concluding with a second major explosion on May 20.

Volcanic ash rained out for more than 150 miles. At a salmon cannery in Chignik 45 miles to the south, every hour of the peak activity brought a pound of dust per square foot. Fishermen reported seeing blocks of pumice the size of water buckets afloat on the ocean.

In June 1931, Father Hubbard, a geologist and fearless explorer of Alaskan volcanoes, returned for his second trip to Aniakchak. A year earlier the caldera had appeared to him as a "plant, fish, and animal world" enclosed by towering walls. Now he found it "a prelude to Hell: black floor, black walls . . . and black vents." On one occasion the volcano spit out not only steam but Father Hubbard and his airplane as well. The party had landed inside the caldera dangerously low on fuel, so low that the plane might not have enough to climb above the walls. Pilot Frank Dorbandt took off, caught a rising thermal, then flew straight for the cone of steam and ash. "We were puffed right into the sky!" recalled Father Hubbard. With the assist from the thermal they cleared the caldera and floated down alongside a fishing boat and borrowed some gas. *(Continued on page 116)*

S edge-covered cinder cone, remnant of Aniakchak's fiery past, rises 200 feet toward a ceiling of mist. Colliding air currents create dense fog; foul weather occurs an average of two out of three days. Often "cloud niagaras" billow in—swift-moving clouds that ride over the crater rim and rush to the floor like water plunging down a precipice.

Bundled in as many as five layers of clothing, campers take refuge from a July downpour. Remote, stormy Aniakchak may prove tough to penetrate, but determined visitors, say park planners, will get there. About 100 did in 1983.

As we hiked to the far side of Vent Mountain, we saw one obvious remnant of those fiery days: an enormous field of lava and black obsidian rock. By contrast, most volcanic rock in Aniakchak had weathered to lighter colors. "There's a lot of variety for the feet here," observed Stacy during a stop for lunch. "At one moment there is pumice rock and then suddenly the ground is firm like asphalt. Then at the next moment you are walking on top of craggy lava formations, then ravines with moss, followed by sedimentary rocks with fossils and rubber-like mud that is covered with algae."

"This place is like a sunken island," Bud added. "Rather than an

JAN ZAHLER SUGAR

island sitting up out of the ocean, it's like an island that sank into the earth. We are surrounded on all sides by rocks and mountains." A hike to the far side of the crater's rim revealed a snowfield protected from the sun and the wind by overhanging rocks. Just by angling the soles of our hiking boots and shifting our body weight forward and backward, we glissaded to the bottom in a quarter of the time required to climb the mountain. Great fun!

During the two-hour hike from Vent Mountain to our camp at Surprise Lake the temperature dropped 20 degrees. Large clouds formed over the valley floor; as small ones took shape on the rim they were swiftly sucked down into the big ones—a science fiction scene.

For the next few days wind-driven rain kept us close to camp. By the fifth day of our trip, eager to get moving, we assembled the two rafts and headed downriver. In little more than an hour the morning's flat calm changed to a snapping squall, the tempo of the river increasing with the fury of the storm. As it flows through the Gates, the river drops turbulently an average of 60 feet a mile for 15 miles (50 feet per mile is regarded as extremely fast water). Then it meanders another 17 miles to Aniakchak Bay and the Pacific Ocean. Wild river, scenic river—aptly enough, the Aniakchak is included in the National Wild and Scenic Rivers System.

During one swift stretch we handlined the rafts; then, at the Gates, Bud, Marc, and Paul ran the empty rafts while the rest of us portaged the gear for more than a mile. After making that walk four times with more than 50 pounds per trip, I was on the verge of hypothermia—a dangerous drop in body temperature. It was the following morning that we awoke near the churning rapids, our sleeping bags awash.

After some discussion we decide to push on. While Paul and Marc's 13-foot raft easily penetrates the standing waves of the rapids, the 16-footer doesn't fare as well. A narrow spot in the river forces the big raft toward a large, flat circular rock. Bud and I try to push off with our oars, but the raft slides to a halt.

Surrounded by raging white water and unable to off-load any gear to lighten the raft, we are stranded. The noise of the wind, the rain, and the rapids only intensifies our dilemma. Jan and Stacy, waiting on shore, shout encouragement but can do nothing to help. After half an hour of rocking and pushing, Bud and I begin to move the raft, inches at a time. As we slide sideways off the rock, we start turning in circles. Bud's right oar strikes a rock, breaking chunks off the blade. Seconds later I try to fend the raft away from the shore with an oar. Instead of pushing off, the blade digs into the soggy embankment. The handle snaps out of my hands. In one swift motion the oar strikes me behind the ear and sends me sprawling across the bow.

For about ten minutes we whirl downriver through angry white water, out of control, hemmed by steep embankments, slamming into rocks, then breaking loose. Finally a shallow, quiet spot appears along one shore, and we steer into it. No serious damage done. Jan and Stacy have tracked us down the same shore—and not without hazard as well. They have scrambled through dense brush in what Stacy recognizes as brown bear terrain. Now we are all back on the river, safely together.

Beyond the rapids, at mile 15, the character of the river changes completely, widening into a braided series of lazy oxbows. No longer tensing for the next rapid, we relax and allow the current to carry us along. Bald eagles appear. Mottled juveniles chase each other through the sky; handsome white-headed adults feed on salmon. Our bird list grows, including rock ptarmigan, snow buntings, water pipits, Lapland longspurs, Barrow's goldeneye ducks, semipalmated plovers. Perhaps this is Aniakchak's reward to us for the hard, threatening days of storm and wild water.

We are so intent on watching the wildlife that none of us realizes how fast the ocean is approaching and the trip ending. "I kept expecting to come out into pounding surf," Stacy says several days later. "Instead we came out into glassy calm. It was a perfect end."

But never too easy.

The hikes through the caldera and the rides on the rapids had thoroughly tested our survival skills. In fact, the lonely, wind-lashed obstacle course of the national monument at Aniakchak typifies the challenge of the Alaskan wilderness, where climate and terrain often force people to live their lives close to the limit. In Aniakchak, as in the rest of Alaska, everything must be earned.

Mossy hillside cushions the author (at left) and his party during a rest stop. A month after the 1931 eruption an observer saw the scarred crater as a "prelude to Hell." Half a century later these travelers found fingers of vegetation reaching out from the moist banks of Surprise Lake and the Aniakchak River. Beyond the high rim spreads four-fifths of the monument area, a realm of spectacular slopes and waterfalls, of coastland where seals and sea lions dwell and fishermen find salmon and king crabs.

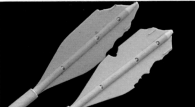

Boiling Aniakchak plays bump-and-run with rafters punching through the Gates. Narrow, shallow, strewn with unforgiving boulders, the river drops 60 feet a mile as it

spills down from the caldera. Swept along by white water, the crew parried the S-turns with oars used both as a rudder and a pry. The two at left bear witness to the battering. After 15 miles the Aniakchak broadens and slows to course a green valley of rolling hills, with eaglets in aeries and brown bears feasting on salmon—a lazy river meandering to the sea.

YUKON-CHARLEY RIVERS

By Tom Melham

THE YUKON RIVER is Alaska's Mason-Dixon line, its meeting place of north and south. It splits the state, leaving portions roughly equal in area but very different in appearance. One half is dominated by the grim and slaty Brooks Range, the other by the snowcapped enormities of the Alaska Range. One tends toward treelessness and caribou, the other toward forests and muskeg and moose. Parts of this river and its tributaries distinguish arctic from subarctic more accurately than does the Arctic Circle line on a map.

In addition, the Yukon's immense watershed delineates Alaska's interior: a generally low-lying heartland hemmed by mountains and as patchworked with rolling hills, woods, and wetlands as it is with tales of sourdoughs past and present. The river is big—1,979 miles long—and its size has made it both barrier and highway. Only one permanent bridge crosses the Yukon in Alaska, yet summer boats and winter sleds have plied this east-west artery for thousands of years. It is not a wilderness stream as much as a Main Street serving scores of widely scattered towns and cabins along its banks.

It is also a river whose history sparkles with the romance of gold. The ore-rich Klondike River that lured thousands nearly a century ago was just one of many Yukon tributaries to yield pay dirt. Jack London and Robert Service spun tales of colorful and often lonely men searching for the mythical mother lode. Mining camps, dance halls, and roadhouses swiftly bloomed, then faded. So did boomtowns like Canada's Dawson and Alaska's Eagle and Circle. Despite its log cabin architecture, Circle proclaimed itself "Paris of the North." Today a more modest Circle (1980 population 81) bears a quieter slogan—"The End of the Road"—reflecting the town's position as the northern terminus of the mostly unpaved Steese Highway that leads to Fairbanks. Until the oil pipeline haul road to Prudhoe Bay was opened to the public in 1983, Circle was the northernmost spot in the nation on an interconnected highway system.

At Circle, some 170 river miles west of the Canadian border, the Yukon broadens into oxbows and braids that mark the start of the topographically drab Yukon Flats. Upstream, it shoulders through much more variable terrain: Steep forested palisades quickly change to bare domes, then to angular hogbacks formed by the uptilting and eroding of ancient strata. Some of the bedrock ranks among the oldest in Alaska, going back perhaps 850 million years. Wildlife abounds, including Dall's sheep, black and brown bears, wolves, wolverines,

Wandering ways of the Charley River take a horseshoe bend pierced by tributary waters of Crescent Creek, about 76 river miles above the Yukon. Ample wildlife roams the Yukon-Charley Rivers preserve, including various birds of prey such as this immature great horned owl (above).

Photographs by Stephen J. Krasemann

121

many smaller mammal species, and eagles, owls, and peregrine falcons. For all these reasons the Alaska portion of the upper Yukon—from just below Eagle to just above Circle—is now within the Yukon-Charley Rivers National Preserve.

"This is the place—*the place*—for peregrines," says Skip Ambrose of the U. S. Fish and Wildlife Service. For ten years now Skip has monitored peregrine populations along the upper Yukon, and after recording five years of downward trends he has some encouraging news. Along the Yukon peregrines have made a comeback. And the success story generally is such that the government plans to change

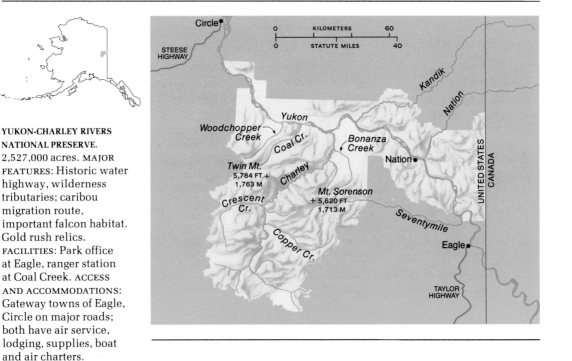

YUKON-CHARLEY RIVERS NATIONAL PRESERVE. 2,527,000 acres. MAJOR FEATURES: Historic water highway, wilderness tributaries; caribou migration route, important falcon habitat. Gold rush relics. FACILITIES: Park office at Eagle, ranger station at Coal Creek. ACCESS AND ACCOMMODATIONS: Gateway towns of Eagle, Circle on major roads; both have air service, lodging, supplies, boat and air charters. ACTIVITIES: River running, cruising, or floating; fishing, wildlife watching; visiting gold rush sites. Sport hunting. FOR INFORMATION: Superintendent, Box 64, Eagle, Alaska 99738.

the species' status over part of its range from endangered to threatened. Skip feels that such a move would be premature. For one thing, although the United States generally banned the use of DDT in 1972, residual amounts remain in the environment. And peregrines migrate yearly to South America, where the pesticide is still in use. Also, there are additional substances in our environment that affect eggshell thickness, and many of these are still being used.

Prized in the sport of falconry, peregrines face another danger: kidnapping. During one survey Skip discovered four chicks missing from a single aerie with no sign of predators. At about the same time an airport baggage handler 200 miles away in Fairbanks accidentally tipped over a pet cage and discovered a hidden panel in the container. The box held the four missing peregrines, and when a man arrived to claim his "dog," he was promptly arrested.

On his field trips Skip plies the Yukon until he nears an aerie or spots adult peregrines. Then he sets out pigeons fitted with back harnesses that have loops of monofilament fishline attached. When a falcon goes for the bait, the loops snare the peregrine's talons. Skip and his assistants then weigh, measure, and band the birds, taking blood and feather samples for chemical analysis. They also climb to the aeries to survey the chicks. Descending, the men scatter moth-balls to mask their scent from foxes and other predators that have learned to identify the smell of humans with easy sources of food.

As we hiked to one aerie, Dr. Ken Riddle, a Texas veterinarian, told of an acquaintance who had been hit by a peregrine near its aerie. Two pounds of feathers, bone, muscle, and determination literally knocked the man out. "He woke up a few minutes later with his face in the dirt," said Ken.

We are more fortunate, reaching the aerie but avoiding the parents. It is not much, just a bare stone ledge devoid of anything like a nest. On it sit three grayish chicks, about 20 days old. I lean to pick one up; its tiny wings flare out and the beak opens in threat. I pocket the animal parts that litter the immediate area; they will document the chicks' diet. Skip identifies the remains in a glance: "Lesser yellow-legs. Jay. Duck. Snipe. Plover. Rabbit fur—that's kind of neat; usually only 2 percent of their diet is mammalian."

Back down we go. A raven flaps by, perhaps 30 feet above the Yu-kon. There is a flash of slate and speckled white as one of the falcon parents makes a classic dive—"stoop" in the idiom of falconry—and the raven is reduced to crumpled feathers, crashing into the river.

In addition to its wildlife the preserve includes the entire water-shed of the Charley River, a Yukon tributary quite unlike its parent stream. While the Yukon is wide and brown, the Charley flows nar-row and clear. Where the Yukon has been a river of commerce and gold seekers, the Charley has remained basically unexploited. Offer-ing visitors a splash or two of white water, plentiful wildlife, and good fishing, the Charley is a fine stream to float.

One problem is the difficulty of access—actually an asset in pro-tecting this wild and scenic river. There is only one primitive land-ing site for fixed-wing aircraft; otherwise, getting to the Charley's upper reaches means either hiring a helicopter or motoring upstream in a shallow-draft boat or raft. My group opted for the chopper. Even so, it took a day to ferry our gear from Circle some 75 air miles away, assemble the raft frames, inflate the rafts, and repack supplies.

The Charley is for the most part a shallow "rock garden," where the danger lies more often in hanging up on a shoal rather than in be-ing swallowed by deep holes or outmuscled by hydraulics. Still, the water flows fast and clear; suspended on its crystalline surface, you watch the river's uneven and shingly pavement race by only inches below. Reddish, black, white, and brown stones sparkle as you pass, evoking the feel of a vast, sunlit mosaic.

Along the banks great flaky crags poke above green slopes like bat-tlements above a castle, and against this backdrop soar both golden and bald eagles. White puffs of Dall's sheep tuft dark knuckles of rock. Two moose calves dawdle on the shore; they are goofy and puppy-like, their ears far too big and floppy even for their elongated heads, the toothpick legs hopelessly fragile beneath such clumsy bodies. They are also too trusting, merely staring as we pass. But soon they will take on adult ways and, like the large bull we spot downriv-er, will trot off into the willow thickets at first sight of humans—or any other potential predators. Because Yukon-Charley is a preserve, it is open to both sport and subsistence hunting and trapping.

For days we have seen tracks of bear, wolf, and porcupine, but not one of these animals in the flesh. Today our luck changes: About a

124

Prime playground for river runners, the Charley offers rugged backdrops, moderate current, and few rapids, but reaching its source usually means a plane or helicopter charter. Bars and shoals dictate the use of shallow-draft vessels such as these inflatable rafts and kayaks—which can serve double duty at rest stops (left).

hundred yards away we spot a black bear. It bashes through some spruces, then starts up a steep slope about 500 feet high. Its gait is leisurely—yet it tops the slope in less than three minutes. The same climb might take me five times as long. I'm always amazed at how slow bears seem—and how quickly they sprint over almost any terrain. They can ford streams and climb trees just as easily, so I was not unhappy to see this bear make the ridge—and disappear.

I cannot claim to be an avid fisherman, only a fair-weather one who enjoys bending a rod from time to time. So it was that, during a break in our journey, I picked out a foam-flecked eddy where plummeting cliffs seemed to promise deep waters.

My first two casts, using a small silvery lure, came back empty. I was already slipping off into a daydream during my third attempt when—bang!—a splash and tug on the line roused me. The battle was brief; a minute later I had the 16-inch-long loser in hand. Its gray,

$\bigvee$inged symbol for environmental causes, the imperiled peregrine falcon still soars above the Yukon—where cliffs and abundant prey support a major nesting area. Peregrine numbers dipped sharply in recent decades, when use of DDT and related pesticides hampered breeding. Monitoring falcons in the preserve, biologist Skip Ambrose scales their aeries to band chicks (below).

Flanked by assistants Tom Nichols and Ken Riddle, Ambrose weighs a mature female, wrapped in protective stocking and hood (right). The team takes other measurements and blood and feather samples before freeing the falcons. The population trend: markedly upward, since the U. S. banned DDT.

126

lightly spotted body and big dorsal fin marked it as grayling. We grilled three that evening over an open fire, their succulent flesh affirming the grayling's reputation as one of Alaska's tastiest fishes.

It is now the second week of June—shirt-sleeve weather in sunshine, but nights are cool enough for down gear. The Charley's steeply channeled watershed magnifies the effects of any rainfall; moderate but daylong showers raise the river level at least a foot. Sections of bank erode, revealing buried lenses of permafrost ice. The next day—our fifth on the Charley—the river twists through hairpin bends and severs some marshy flats. Finally it enters what appears to be a large but fast-moving lake: We have reached the Yukon.

Eyes that have grown accustomed to banks 30 or 40 yards apart now must expand horizons to fit the Yukon's half-mile width, hemmed between sheer bluffs and spattered with low islands. Despite steady head winds, our rowing helps us manage 8 to 10 miles an hour downstream. Occasional log cabins punctuate the riverside, some apparently used at least seasonally, some obviously derelict. Just offshore sits a fish wheel—a rotating wooden seine that turns with the river's current, scooping up whatever happens to be going upstream. Nothing now, but in another three weeks or so fish wheels churning the Yukon will harvest the July run of king salmon.

There is ice here, too, not like the Charley's hidden lenses but hefty, automobile-size chunks instead. Blackened by repeated brawls and elbow-rubbings with the Yukon's banks, these remnants have floated here from as far as hundreds of miles away. They are relics of spring breakup, the yearly apocalypse that usually occurs in May, when thawing river ice splits into enormous pieces. Rising waters surge down each feeder stream, and crunching torrents of ice and melt converge. Vast jams pile up and break loose, bulldozing whatever lies in the way. Eventually the runoff peaks and recedes, stranding leftover ice on shore. The momentum of breakup leaves other reminders as well—ridges of black mud 10 or 12 feet high, and uprooted trees strewn on the ground like pickup sticks.

There is a grandness to the Yukon River that transcends its size. Views are varied and unhindered, colors muted but rich. Greens and blues—trees, water, and sky—predominate, while rock cliffs rise in layered pastels much like the walls of the Grand Canyon.

"There's a tranquillity here, a magnificence," says Dr. Carol Allison, a University of Alaska paleontologist and frequent visitor to the area. "You get on the upper Yukon and it gets in your blood. It's home to me; it's the best part of Alaska."

When a Yukon-Charley Rivers preserve was first proposed, some local residents feared it would mean they could no longer hunt, trap, or prospect as they always had. They worried that development would result, bringing more outsiders and more changes. But in the first three years of the preserve's existence none of the residents' fears have been realized. Superintendent Dave Mihalic has gained respect for sensitivity to the concerns of local people as well as the land. For example, he located the preserve headquarters in an existing Eagle building, rather than erect a new structure that would generate complaints about development. He recruited three seasonal rangers locally—despite the fact that all three at first opposed the preserve. He did so partly because he valued their backwoods expertise, partly in hopes of overcoming the "We-versus-They" mentality.

Gold in the birches gleams at Woodchopper Creek. Gray windrows of tailings mark the hunt for gold in the ground that still draws miners to Yukon tributaries. The waterways enable crews to sift vast tonnages for relatively tiny amounts of placer gold. Dredging here has churned through some 2.5 miles of creek gravels.

FOLLOWING PAGES: Pebbled shores of the Charley wend quietly to the Yukon. Bereft of gold, this tributary remains pristine— virtually undisturbed by man along its 120-mile course.

The trio's opposition originally stemmed from a belief that the Park Service would restrict hunting, fishing, and trapping—activities on which they and many other Eagle residents relied for their subsistence. Today they still hunt, fish, and trap. The three rangers now see the Park Service—and their own participation—as beneficial to the area. They're even becoming downright proprietary.

"Our role," one told me, "is not to protect you but to protect the land. You've got to watch out for yourself."

This, of course, is what residents have done for years. It is excellent advice for visitors. For good reason: Yukon-Charley is as remote and undeveloped now as it was before the preserve was established. In fact, the area is wilder today than it was 80 years ago, when the valley was much more densely populated, the land more creased with trails, and when roadhouses rose along the Yukon at 20-mile intervals. The fact that the Park Service has not installed any facilities or trails here has gained it increasing local support.

Says Dave Mihalic, "The comment I hear most often from local people is, 'Leave it like it is.' That's just what we're trying to do."

BERING
LAND BRIDGE

By Tom Melham

I AM STARING AT A BIT OF HISTORY, and history is staring right back. On the sand before me lies a human skull, weathered and lichen-encrusted, one eye socket sheltering a tiny cranberry plant. Not 20 yards away breakers crash and froth timelessly against the shore. My map shows no name for this desolate barrier island, one of about a dozen that shield the northwestern edge of the Seward Peninsula from the forbidding Chukchi Sea.

It is mid-July and, although I am only 50 miles south of the Arctic Circle, temperatures hold to the 70s. Skies are blue, the sunlight so brilliant that it seems to hammer this land as flat as the ocean. Fifty miles offshore sit the rocky Diomede Islands, shared by the United States and the U.S.S.R.; 30 miles farther is Siberia.

The skull seems at once old and new; its lichens argue for age, while its position—on the surface, not even partly buried—makes it appear a recent addition. Not likely. A short walk brings me to sun-bleached whale ribs arching up from the beach—the traditional sign-post here for a burial place. Human bones show through the cracked wooden roofs of shallow graves. Scattered about are a rusted shot-gun, whale vertebrae, a decayed kayak paddle, and a strap-on ice skate. Nearby, beach erosion exposes a midden, an old trash pit, filled with seal bones from long-ago feasts. T-shaped mounds, rough-ly 7 by 15 feet, indicate remains of Eskimo dwellings.

These vestiges of settlement have never been excavated by archae-ologists. This is both a strength and a weakness. On one hand the lack of excavation lends an isolated feel to the land. Everything is just here, as time left it. But everything also is exposed to the whims of man and nature. Holes already pock some dunes, evidence that pot hunters have been here. The Park Service outlaws pot hunting but cannot always prevent it. Steve Christy, who has served as an investi-gator for the Bureau of Indian Affairs—the agency charged with veri-fying Native historic sites throughout Alaska—deplores the pot hunting and would love to organize a dig here. He believes the site contains shards of successive villages, some parts dating at least to the 17th century—decades before Bering, Cook, Kotzebue, and other explorers reached these shores.

Seward Peninsula harbors many significant relics of Alaska's past, but the biggest and most remarkable is the peninsula itself. Like Sibe-ria's Chukotskiy, Seward is a stubby remnant of Beringia—an isth-mus that periodically linked North America to Asia while it cut off

Weathered granite tors seem to trudge across a rolling landscape of the Seward Peninsula. In Ice Age days the land ran unbroken to Asia. A curious musk-ox (above)—its species little changed since the Ice Age—ventured within ten feet of the photographer. Killed off in Alaska, then reintroduced, musk-oxen today number about 1,200 in the state.

Photographs by Tim Thompson

133

BERING LAND BRIDGE NATIONAL PRESERVE. 2,785,000 acres. MAJOR FEATURES: Archaeological sites, flowering tundra, volcanic landscape, beaches, sea cliffs; marine and land mammals, migratory water birds. FACILITIES: None. ACCESS AND ACCOMMODATIONS: Air charters, lodging, supplies at Kotzebue, Nome. Primitive road from Nome to Taylor. ACTIVITIES: Wildlife watching, visiting hot springs, wilderness camping, sport hunting. FOR INFORMATION: Superintendent, Box 220, Nome, Alaska 99762.

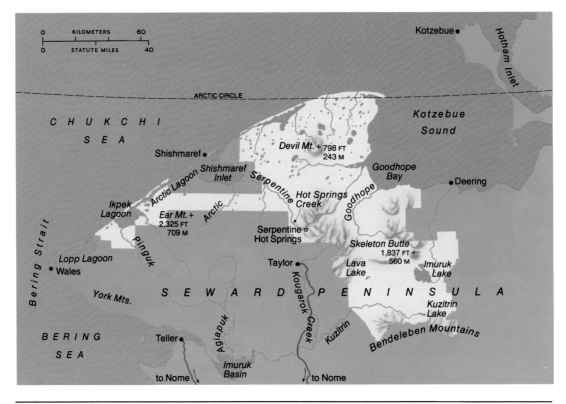

the Arctic Ocean from the Pacific. Beringia—also known as the Bering Land Bridge—commemorates Vitus Bering, the Danish discoverer of Alaska in 1741. Bering was chosen in 1724 by Russia's Peter the Great to determine whether Asia and North America were connected. In 1648 Semyon Dezhnev had already determined that they weren't, but his report was gathering dust in a Siberian outpost.

The Beringian land was first submerged 3½ million years ago. Then, during the Ice Age—the Pleistocene epoch—huge ice sheets locked up so much water that sea levels fell several hundred feet worldwide. Bering Strait again became dry land. Old World plants and animals, including mastodons, lemmings, and musk-oxen, invaded the Americas. So did their human hunters, ancestors of today's Indians.

During relatively warm interglacial periods the ice melted and seas rose. North America broke with Asia; oceans united, and marine life took its turn at migrating. Sea urchins, for example, slowly extended their range from Pacific to Atlantic via Arctic waters. But with the next glacial advance Beringia returned, variously evolving as tundra, marsh, and rocky, sparsely vegetated terrain.

We are now in the most recent interglacial, which began 10,000 to 14,000 years ago; but sizable portions of the former land bridge remain above water. With the Alaska Lands Act of 1980 part of it became the Bering Land Bridge National Preserve.

"A lot of people take that to mean submerged parts of Beringia," says Superintendent Larry Rose. "I'm frequently asked, 'How do you manage all that land under water?' "

Actually, preserve boundaries extend only to mean high tide. Perhaps a more basic problem with the name is that "bridge" implies a narrow conduit for moving traffic, when in fact the land bridge extended across thousands of square miles. At its maximum extent, 18,000 years ago, Beringia was 850 miles wide. It was more a place, a recurring subcontinent, than merely a connective thread.

Today's preserve stretches from land's end to the squat Bendeleben Mountains. Its odd shape results from the granting of sizable land tracts to Natives of Shishmaref and other Seward Peninsula villages. Bush pilot Tom Falley is impressed by the depth of contrast in this bleak realm: "It's got very big things—tremendous open spaces and great scenics—and very tiny details—lichens and flowers and patterns in the rocks. There's no middle ground."

Most of it is tundra, fairly flat yet full of a quiet beauty far different from Alaska's towering spectacles. Flying over it flattens it even more, but wait—what are those brown lumps, seemingly legless, humping along like dry-land porpoises? A closer look reveals hooves poking out just beneath the shaggy canopies of brown hair. They are musk-oxen, living and breathing leftovers from Pleistocene assemblages that included mammoths and mastodons.

Unlike caribou, musk-oxen don't go on long migrations in search of food, says Dr. David Klein, a University of Alaska mammalogist. They tend to stay in one place, surviving on twigs and tough grasses that caribou can't handle. Long guard hairs protect them from the insects that send caribou into a frenzied gallop. When predators threaten, musk-oxen usually stand their ground, shouldering together into a circle, facing outward in a nearly impenetrable buttress of horns.

It's a great defense against wolves, says Klein. But not against man. Hunters apparently wiped out the musk-ox in Siberia a few thousand years ago. The arrival of firearms finished off Alaska's herds in the 19th century; the animal persisted only in the most remote Arctic regions—Greenland and extreme northern Canada.

Musk-oxen returned to Alaska in 1930, not by land bridge but by boat and train: Scientists decided to reintroduce experimentally a few dozen animals from Greenland. They prospered, so much so that some were also reestablished in Siberia. Often considered gentle or even stupid, this long-haired cousin of the water buffalo can fight fiercely when provoked. Klein says one of his students witnessed a confrontation between a bull and a grizzly: "The bear charged, chasing the bull a couple of hundred yards, gaining on it. Suddenly the bull stopped, turned, pawed the ground, and took off after the grizzly! You know, the bear turned tail—beaten by a 'gentle' musk-ox."

About 200 musk-oxen roam the Seward Peninsula today, as do the descendants of another import: (Continued on page 140)

Purple Kamchatka rhododendron—rare in Alaska, common in Siberia—glows across the tundra near Serpentine Hot Springs. The gravelly soil, underlain with permafrost, supports grasses and sedges, lichens and mosses— 245 plant species but no trees across the 2.8 million acres. Migratory birds from seven continents find nesting habitat here. And to the springs come bathers, some with ills they hope will soak away in the sulfurous waters.

Fringe of floes, residue of spring breakup of the Chukchi Sea pack ice, lingers into July along a barrier island in the preserve. Ikpek Lagoon lies blue in the background. Along the coast archaeologists have explored the remains of an old village with collapsed houses and graves such as the one at left. Heavy driftwood planks, now covered with lichens, roofed the burial place. Upright whale ribs form the traditional symbol here for an Eskimo grave.

the reindeer. This smaller and more easily domesticated version of the caribou was brought here from the Old World to provide a reliable food source for Natives as well as for missionaries, miners, and other newcomers. At times reindeer herding brought profits, but not to the Natives. It also resulted in badly overgrazed tundra, increased animal disease, and range disputes between white herders and Natives. A 1937 law sought to resolve such problems by restricting ownership of the animals to Natives. Today Native owners in the region are trying to make reindeer a profitable industry that will yield both meat and cash. In addition to their own land they enjoy grazing rights to millions of acres, including part of the Bering preserve.

Visitors to the preserve run a chance of seeing reindeer and perhaps caribou. Like most Alaskan national parklands, however, Bering has no visitor facilities, displays, or tours. Access is by air charter or snow machine—or foot—although a five-hour ride over a dirt road from Nome enables four-wheel-drive vehicles to approach one nook of the preserve.

That area includes dramatic Serpentine Hot Springs, surrounded by steep hills edged with jagged, granite outcrops that vary from Stonehenge-like slabs to twisted spines to rows of sharks' teeth. Sulfurous waters measuring 132°F bubble up from a hand-size hole in the valley floor. Metal pipe that predates the preserve carries the waters to a "bathhouse"—a shed-covered pool. The pool receives similar plumbing from frigid Serpentine Creek. Users adjust the water temperature by stuffing rags in either or both of the pipes. Popular for decades among Eskimos as well as whites, Serpentine still draws Native healers and their followers, who regard its pungent waters as remedy for everything from ulcers to infertility.

Serpentine's outcroppings may signify more than scenic curiosities. Travis Hudson, a project geologist for Anaconda Minerals Company, explained that these weird shapes are eroded remnants of magma—molten rock—that rose within the earth and crystallized about 70 million years ago. Just east of the springs placer deposits of the ore-mineral cassiterite were found during gold mining decades ago. Cassiterite is a chief source of tin, but park officials say no one knows if there is enough of it in the parkland to be worth mining.

Magma of a different sort repeatedly punched through the surface near Imuruk Lake as far back as 6 million years ago and as recently as 1,600. The billowy tundra here is blistered with cinder cones. Great rippled sheets and ropes of lava lie cracked into jigsaw puzzle shapes. But this congealed wasteland is not a lifeless one. Walk over it and ptarmigan burst from hiding. You may also find wolf scat near whitening caribou bones. Migratory birds from every continent converge on this fairly open, fairly wet wilderness.

So do mosquitoes. They breed in the damp tundra, where a human footfall looses an instant fog of them. They are Alaska's black snow, the blizzards of summer. They circle like enraged Indians around a wagon train, waiting for your bug dope to wear thin or some chink to show in your cloth armor. Head nets are not affectation here but necessity, especially following a rain.

Alaska mosquitoes are legendary, some large enough to prompt T-shirts showing a mosquito as "Alaska's State Bird." There is no escape. A single slap may kill scores of them, yet always more appear. I conceive a new vision of hell: a five-minute stroll through Imuruk

Reindeer rounded up by helicopter bunch together in a corral near the preserve. When caribou grew scarce in northwest Alaska, the missionary Sheldon Jackson in 1892 imported the closely related reindeer of the Old World and sought to turn Eskimos from hunting to herding for much-needed meat. Reindeer could also haul sleds. The herds swelled, then declined. Some animals defected to wild bands of caribou. Alaska today has some 35,000 reindeer—many of which graze in the Bering preserve.

Lake's tussocks, right after a rain, in dead calm, with no clothes on.

North of the lake the land rears up in a cinder cone named Skeleton Butte. Its summit is only 816 feet above Imuruk, but like Wyoming's rugged Wind River Range or the soaring Canadian Rockies, it forms part of a continental divide. Although usually associated with craggy summits, a divide merely defines different watersheds. The highlands here segregate Chukchi Sea from Bering Sea drainages.

Scaling Skeleton Butte turns out to be some of the easiest hiking I have experienced in Alaska—no alder or willow thickets and few tussocks. The broken lava provides excellent traction. Abruptly I find a series of pits, two or three feet deep and up to ten feet in diameter, carpeted with grasses and delicate tundra flowers. Some pits are lined with lava rocks carefully turned on edge. Upslope a bit stand four cairns, their stones stacked so precisely that humans must have built them. The tallest rises more than five feet, larger at the top than the base. What do the cairns signify? Some sort of monument or burial marker? Perhaps a device for sighting game or gauging distances?

Some day experts may finally decipher the mystery. But even if

they do, these odd little rock piles will continue to symbolize Beringia's eternal lure: that this is where man has lived for at least 12,000 years. And despite this long tenure, nature remains the area's primary architect and engineer. From atop Skeleton Butte I can scan nature's lava-strewn realm for many miles. But always my eyes return to the cairns. There is a magnetism to them, a tingle of excitement in their human origins, a sense of discovery. I am standing right where the mysterious cairn builders stood, seeing what their eyes saw. The past is but an arm's length away, totally exposed, yet still shrouded—just as it was on that lonely barrier island several weeks ago, where I stumbled upon that weathered skull.

Milling through a haze of dust, reindeer move from a main corral to smaller holding pens before passing into a chute for dehorning. Although the herds' most important product remains their meat, the summer roundup takes place to harvest the animals' new antlers, with their velvet cover and spongy interior—much in demand in powdered form for Oriental medicines. Biggest importer: South Korea.

A young herder, at left, wrestles a reluctant animal toward the chute. About three-fourths of all Alaskan reindeer belong to the herds of the Seward Peninsula.

CAPE KRUSENSTERN

By Tom Melham

IN A WAY, it's another Mount McKinley. Cape Krusenstern doesn't have the elevation, of course—it's a gravelly elbow of land barely above sea level, as pocked with saltwater lagoons and brackish ponds as Jarlsberg cheese is with holes. But like Alaska's most famous mountain, it was named for a man who never saw it.

Indeed, Adam Johann von Krusenstern, who led the first Russian expedition to circumnavigate the globe (1803-06), never laid eyes on any part of Alaska. But Otto von Kotzebue, a teenager on that voyage, later explored the Alaska coast and in 1816 bestowed his former commander's name upon this flat interface of land and sea. By the way, Kotzebue didn't land here either. He just sailed by.

If he had gone ashore he might have noticed scores of gravel ridges curving along the beach just south and east of the cape. The ridges remain to this day, and it is primarily because of them that some 658,000 acres here are now a national monument. Krusenstern's ridges contain not only gravel but also ancient house pits, weapons, tools, bones, and other remnants of human history. More than half a dozen distinct cultures, culminating in today's Eskimo, have made the cape their home. They differed in detail but shared some common traits: All lived at the sea's edge, usually in partly subterranean homes built of sod and driftwood; and they fashioned tools and weapons from bone, ivory, antler, and stone.

Krusenstern looks out on an important migratory route of walruses and beluga whales, as well as ringed, bearded, and spotted harbor seals. For thousands of years the appearance of these mammals each spring has lured hunters here. For thousands of years, also, major storms have pounded the cape, each piling up gravel that extended the beach and left a telltale ridge parallel to the surf. Each new extension prompted the hunters to relocate their camps, usually atop the most recent ridge; their livelihood required an unobstructed view of the sea. Today Krusenstern is a corduroy of 114 ridges; its present shoreline lies as much as two miles to seaward of where it was 4,500 years ago. Had the coast not migrated, the hunters probably would have remained in place—and the shards of their cultures would not be so clearly segregated now.

Since major storms and their ridge-spawning waves seem to occur here at intervals of 60 to 90 years or so, the 114 beach ridges constitute an unbroken record of human use—making the area a primary benchmark for Arctic archaeology. What makes it even more special

Artfully carved ivory goggles shielded eyes against ice glare when Ipiutak people hunted at Krusenstern some 2,000 years ago. For six millennia bounties of sea mammals have sustained a continuous chain of subsistence cultures here. Day's catch for a modern sea hunter, a beluga whale lies tethered to shore near the beach camp of Sheshalik—"place of white whales."

Photographs by Tim Thompson

is its horizontal layout. Most archaeological sites are like layer cakes, with newer sediments lying on top of older ones. At Krusenstern, however, archaeologists reach the oldest deposits not by digging deeper but by walking farther inland. The advantages are many: Artifacts are fairly near the surface; excavators need not dig through newer deposits, disturbing them, to reach the old; and there is little mixing of old and new, as often occurs at "vertical" sites.

Low and largely overgrown, the ridges tend to blur together when seen from ground level. But get up in the air, and they stand out clearly, like ocean waves frozen in time, one set of furrows angling into

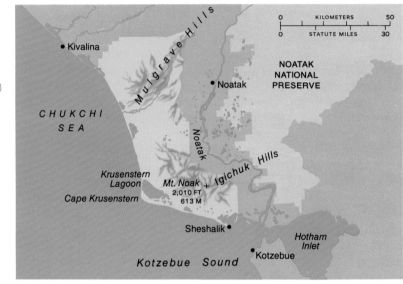

CAPE KRUSENSTERN NATIONAL MONUMENT. 658,000 acres. MAJOR FEATURES: Archaeological beach sites, tundra ecology, wild coast. FACILITIES: Park office at Kotzebue. ACCESS AND ACCOMMODATIONS: Air, boat charters, lodging, supplies at Kotzebue. ACTIVITIES: Wilderness camping; observing marine mammals, tundra wildlife. FOR INFORMATION: Superintendent, Box 287, Kotzebue, Alaska 99752.

the next. It is as if a giant rake had been drawn along the shore, not in one smooth pull but in several short, overlapping strokes.

Airplanes offer not only the best view but also a convenient form of access to the monument, which provides visitors with neither transportation nor tours nor other facilities. So it was that I chartered a plane from Kotzebue, northwest Alaska's unofficial capital. With me was Dr. Douglas Anderson, a Brown University archaeologist who has studied Krusenstern's ridges since 1960. He began as a graduate student with the late Dr. J. Louis Giddings, whose name is to this region what Louis Leakey's is to East Africa.

"See that reddish limestone?" Anderson shouted above the engine's droning as he pointed to some palisades inland of the beach ridges. "That's a 6,000-year-old site." Currently it ranks among the area's oldest, although Anderson believes far older ones eventually will be discovered. "And there—that ridge is where we found evidence of the earliest known whaling in the world," he pointed again. "It's 3,300 to 3,500 years old."

Minutes later we touched down at a local "airstrip"—a smooth stretch of beach gravel. A short walk across the ridges took us to another age, to squarish mounds that represent 2,000-year-old house pits of the Ipiutak culture. We paused at one ruin that was some 20 feet square—enormous compared to its neighbors.

146

"This was my first really spectacular excavation," Anderson mused. "You could tell it had burned down. Inside, right under the smoke hole, I found the ash outline of a human body, with an arrow stuck in the hip. And over here, the outlines of two kids, only four or five years old, also caught in the fire. They had adzes in their hands; you could just see how they were trying to dig out under the house."

In addition to capturing this dramatic moment, the site yielded stone blades, other tools, and "one of our best artifacts—the snow goggles." Anderson proudly showed me an ancient piece of ivory, browned by time but exquisitely carved. An etched tear duct graced the edge of each eyehole; curvilinear designs bordered the entire piece. The holes were deliberately small, he explained, to restrict the amount of light entering and thereby prevent snow blindness, a constant peril to hunters on glaring pack ice. "Originally it would have been pure white," he added. "It must have been striking."

It still is, especially considering that the tools responsible for its delicacy and grace were mere bits of chipped stone. Anderson displayed some Ipiutak tools and weapons: spear points and adzes, and drills that might have been used in making sleds or snowshoes. Some were decorated, demonstrating both a love of art and enough leisure to create it. Obviously, the Ipiutak did not live by meat alone.

In fact, Anderson could not suggest any purpose other than art for the next two treasures he held up, both Ipiutak, made 2,000 years ago. One was threaded and looked like an ivory rendition of a stove bolt. The other was a three-link chain, carved from a single chunk of ivory. "It's awfully hard to imagine someone sitting down with a solid piece of ivory and naturally thinking of making a chain—unless he had seen something like it before," said Anderson. "But where did the Ipiutak see bolts or chains?"

This little mystery, he added, was one of many here. Altogether, about a hundred sites at Krusenstern have been "tested"—excavated at least in part—while hundreds more remain untouched. At least by archaeologists. A hole in one beach ridge caught Anderson's eye.

"Somebody's pulled a bone out here," he said, lamenting the increase in grave looting. "That didn't happen much in the '60s because there were very strong religious sanctions against it. But those old values are breaking down now, and pilfering is going on."

Local people and Park Service officials, however, blame the outside world for creating a lucrative artifact market, and insist that outsiders have been directly involved in rifling the sites. Krusenstern's superintendent, Mack Shaver, plans to assign a ranger to the beach ridges for the entire ice-free season, primarily to protect the relics.

In addition, much of the monument's beachfront—including its ridges—soon will be transferred to Native ownership, the result of long-standing laws designed to give Natives title to traditional hunting grounds. This change could limit excavation but may benefit archaeology, for it could help preserve the sites while new techniques for excavating and analyzing artifacts evolve.

Many Native land transfers within the monument involve Sheshalik, a gravelly, treeless spit that juts into Kotzebue Sound. Here, at ocean's edge, stand plywood and canvas camps—the summer homes of more than a hundred Eskimos. To strangers Sheshalik may seem tumbledown, but to the residents it is a land of milk and honey.

"It's a great food-gathering place," says Bob Uhl, who first came

FOLLOWING PAGES:
Fretwork of lakes and sloughs borders Krusenstern Lagoon; beyond, the Chukchi Sea's unbroken expanse mirrors a moody June sky. By late summer wave-driven gravel dams block tidal outflow from the lagoon, transforming it into a natural fish trap and the site of abundant autumn whitefish harvests.

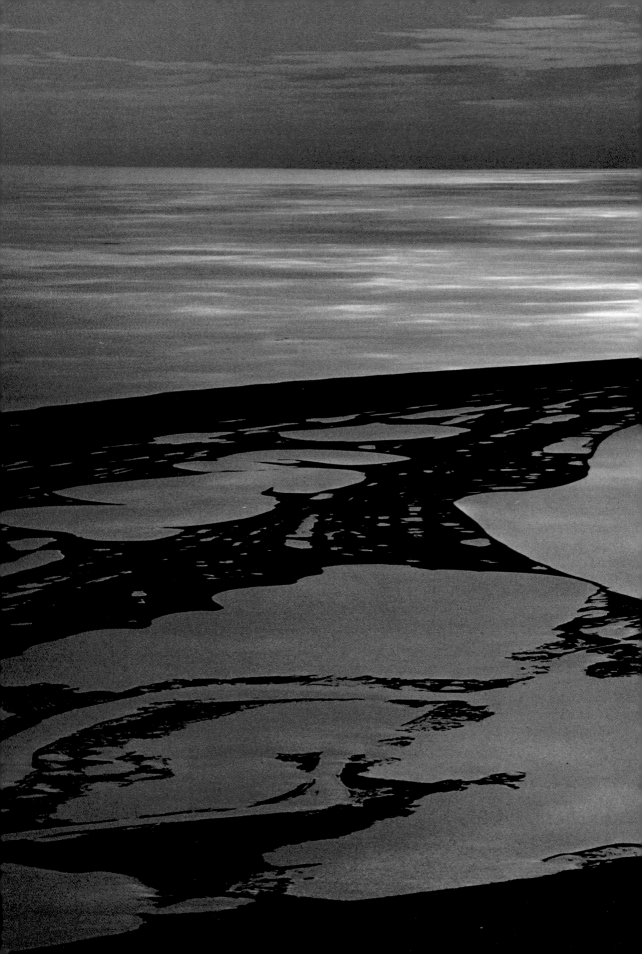

here in 1948 to live with his Eskimo bride. "We get seals, fish, berries, wild celery, ducks, snowshoe hares, and ptarmigan; moose, caribou, and other game are just inland. Everything goes by here on parade. Nothing stays very long, not even the people." Around October, he explains, most residents retreat to villages or inland camps.

Winter's wind chill can make Sheshalik feel a numbing -150°F, says Uhl, and there are no stores, no utilities or doctors or entertainment, apart from an occasional radio. Nor any trees; so firewood is limited mainly to the drift brought by spring floods. Other supplies come by boat or plane from Kotzebue.

It is one price paid for the life-style here, an intriguing mix of old and new. Inside the camps down-filled comforters and caribou hides often warm the same bed. Breakfast cereal and freeze-dried coffee share a shelf with seal oil and dried fish. High-powered rifles, steel knives, and nylon nets long ago replaced traditional hunting weapons, just as snow machines and motorboats have made dog teams and kayaks obsolete. Most of today's technology is the white man's, even in this traditional Eskimo enclave. And yet, the basic Eskimo activities—living off the land and sea, traveling seasonally in quest of food, and other cultural aspects—remain very much alive.

Witness the preparation and enjoyment of such Native gastronomic delights as uilaq. The recipe is simplicity itself: Take fresh whitefish, abundant and easily netted here. Do not scale, gut, or cook; just place in a burlap sack. Let sit outside for about eight months. Serve.

Eating it, I found, can be more involved than making it. When Bob, his wife, Carrie, and two nephews sat down to a platter of uilaq, they followed an almost ritualized sequence. First, each grabbed a knife and sharpened it carefully. Step two was to take a fish—scaled and rinsed minutes before—and draw the blade lightly across its skin, squeegeeing off remaining scales and water. Everyone then surgically subdivided the fare, deftly avoiding bones, tail, fins, and the well-rotted innards. The next step was to dip each chunk in seal oil—the local equivalent of melted butter—and pop it into the mouth. Finally, all sat back and savored, happily comparing the merits of this year's uilaq to previous batches.

It was reminiscent of wine lovers sampling a prized bottle of Lafite-Rothschild, 1947. Indeed, many Eskimos feel that seal oil and other traditional foods improve with age, as fine wines do. Says Bob: "Everybody here goes just crazy over a piece of bowhead whale blubber that's been lying in the sea for a while. It's like aged cheese."

Bob's words—and actions—reflect the 6,000-year-old human heritage of Krusenstern: survival by relying on local plants and animals. It is a tradition, "a living history lesson," says Mack Shaver, that the Park Service seeks to preserve. This privilege of subsistence use extends not only to people on private allotments within the parks, but also to residents of areas legally defined as "local and rural," explained Mack. "The idea is to include people who may live in towns but traditionally have relied on the park for much of their food."

In a statewide referendum in November 1982, voters dramatically reaffirmed the privileges of subsistence users. But the issue remains controversial and has spawned a vocal opposition. "Subsistence is just another word for favoritism," barked a Fairbanks accountant, who considers hunting to be the birthright of all Alaskans. Never mind that he and other sport hunters can hunt legally throughout most of the state. He still resents laws that ban him from the same national parklands that are open to subsistence hunters.

Others point out that subsistence hunting, like sport hunting, involves a certain amount of wasteful killing. "While waste is against the law, it occurs," admits Mack Shaver, although he feels it is not a major concern, at least at Cape Krusenstern.

He estimates that there were some 26,000 visits to Krusenstern in 1982, most by subsistence users. Perhaps a hundred were outsiders visiting this new national monument. Park planners foresee no great increase, nor any pressure for development. But times can change, and even Bob Uhl, whose wife will become a landowner at Sheshalik, voiced concern over future changes that private ownership might encourage: "New homes already are being built on Sheshalik," he said, "and here one new house changes the whole horizon. You can see it seven or eight miles away."

One technique for protecting the parklands is the recently developed Alaska Land Bank Program. It offers participants tax benefits and free federal maintenance of their lands in return for a "preservation easement" that would bar commercial development. Will the program succeed? It is too early to tell.

The only certainty is that Alaska's parklands will seek to preserve not only the land, plants, and animals, but a traditional life-style as well. The life-style of people like Bob Uhl, who recalled his early days at Sheshalik: "I used to climb those mountains," he said, pointing to distant hills toward the Noatak River. "I'd go up there, and all I could see was mine. You had real freedom then, no one to tell you what to do. And the land—" his voice broke. "I'm talking about what I love more than anything on earth—this is my *home!*"

For Bob's sake, and for the monument's, I hope that preservation succeeds—and that developers will follow Otto von Kotzebue's example: Look, but pass on by.

S weep of history at Cape Krusenstern advances seaward along parallel ridges shaped successively by ocean storms. Each ridge once marked the shoreline, the site of hunting camps. In their remains archaeologists such as Dr. Douglas Anderson (at left, above, with the author) read a detailed record of the past.

Halcyon days at Sheshalik: Spring and summer usher in flurries of fishing and hunting as ice-out frees the waters. "Everything goes by here on parade," says Bob Uhl (in parka, dining with guests), a Californian wedded to the Eskimo life. June sunshine speeds the drying of char, a staple food fish. Lena Sours packs blubber of bearded seal— a delicacy after it ages for a spell. Most valued of marine mammals in traditional culture, this seal also yields meat, gut, and hide for food, boats, and clothing.

KOBUK VALLEY

By Tom Melham

THERE IS AN EMPTINESS to tundra, an aching, pit-of-the-stomach emptiness born of its low profile and its treelessness, but mostly of its sheer size. Even when it ripples with gentle rises and troughs, it feels empty and flat, pressed down by the huge sky above.

I am between tundra and boreal forest, in a narrow transition zone tufted with scrawny birches. Behind me, spruce-crowded bluffs plunge to the Kobuk River and beyond. Ahead, the utterly treeless tundra sprawls clear to the Arctic Ocean some 270 miles away. I can see about ten of those miles, to the humpbacked Jade Mountains on the northern horizon. The land is so bare and the air so crystalline that the Jades stand out as sharp and clear as the blueberries at my feet. This despite a gauzy curtain of falling snow—the season's first.

Strange to see snow when only two weeks ago it was August. But this is the Arctic, where summer can suddenly give way to cold winds and rain. Yesterday was such a day, and last night the rain began to freeze. Now, at midday, the big wet flakes are still coming down, starting to take hold on the soggy tundra, plastering over its hollows and making it flatter, even emptier, even more beautiful.

Suddenly there is a rattling of branches. I look toward the noise—and freeze. Amid some birches not 50 feet away, two large brown eyes are staring right at me. Cautiously an antlered head emerges, followed by the neck, body, and legs of a bull caribou.

There is not a shrub or boulder between us, and my bright yellow oilskins make poor camouflage. But the bull ignores me and moves on. Instantly other caribou burst from the birches, following their leader, apparently coming up from lower ground. Soon there are dozens, then hundreds, then thousands—streaming past me, some as close as ten yards, a churning tide of gray coats and graceful, curving antlers. Bulls, cows, yearlings, and calves all are intermixed, one great mega-organism oozing across the tundra like floodwaters over a levee. I am entranced. Minutes ago the land was bare; now it throbs with a spectacular procession of life.

Eventually the lead caribou—by now about half a mile off—stops, and his companions begin to lie down, apparently to rest. Seconds later I hear, from another direction, distant gunfire. As additional volleys echo across the emptiness, the caribou calmly rise and go back on parade, flowing off toward the far side of a low ridge. They do not stampede; most do not even trot. Even so, the thousands are gone in what seems only seconds, vanished as if they had never been.

Autumn's gold paints trees and tundra in mountain-rimmed Kobuk Valley, a center of the Native lifeway called niqi malikaat— they followed the meat. Highway for fishermen and hunters, the Kobuk offers an abundance of caribou, moose, fish, berries—and birch bark (above) for basketry, a craft that lives on in the changing Arctic.

Photographs by Tim Thompson

Such is the magic of Kobuk Valley National Park, a 1.7-million-acre showcase that includes tundra, forest, mountains, valleys, the most extensive moving sand dunes in Arctic North America—and not one mile of road. Thousands of lakes and streams feed the park's namesake river. Although the name means "great river" in Eskimo, the Kobuk is puny compared to the Yukon or other northern arteries. But it has been since prehistoric times an important food source and a major east-west highway for Arctic people. Some 60 of its 280 miles fall within the park, which also embraces the entire Salmon River, a Kobuk tributary and a National Wild and Scenic River.

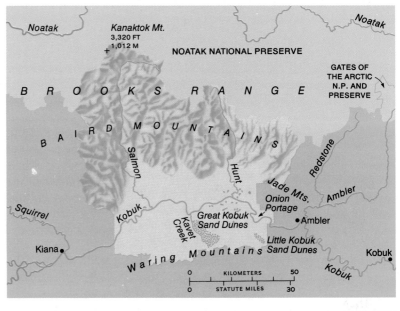

KOBUK VALLEY NATIONAL PARK. 1,750,000 acres. MAJOR FEATURES: Wilderness streams, migrating caribou, Arctic sand dunes, relics of ancient settlements. FACILITIES: Park office at Kotzebue, ranger station at Onion Portage. ACCESS AND ACCOMMODATIONS: Air charters at Kotzebue, Ambler. Lodging, supplies at Kotzebue. Boat charters at Ambler, Kiana. ACTIVITIES: Float trips, fishing, dune hiking, backpacking, wildlife watching. FOR INFORMATION: Superintendent, Box 287, Kotzebue, Alaska 99752.

I was on the Kobuk's north bank, just inside the park's eastern boundary, when the caribou staged their appearing/disappearing act. The area is called Onion Portage, partly for its wild onions and partly because river travelers have long known they could trim five or six miles here by crossing the neck of a Kobuk oxbow.

The caribou arrive each autumn, as their scattered bands on the tundra coalesce into larger and larger groups and head south toward the subarctic woodlands where they winter. Many thousands cross the Kobuk at Onion Portage. Their arrival here precipitates a second coming—that of the Eskimos, who rely on caribou as their mainstay through the long winter. Rather than stalk the animals over open tundra, hunters usually await them in the river where they can be easily approached, shot, and snagged from boats. This hunt is no sporting event; it is the seasonal harvesting of a vital food. It is also legal in the park, because it is a traditional subsistence activity.

Late summer and autumn represent a glorious time of plenty in Kobuk Valley, the time not only of caribou but also of whitefish and sheefish and salmon, tons of which are netted as they surge upriver to spawn. It is also the time when the ducks and geese that breed here gather in vast flocks for their annual flights south, and when ripening blueberries, salmonberries, and cranberries fill the tundra—as well as many human stomachs. Such seasonal abundance at Onion Portage has long made it a favorite food-gathering area. And because of this it is an archaeological gold mine today.

The late Dr. J. Louis Giddings of Brown University excavated the site—which one scholar has called "the small end of a funnel" both for animals and man as they moved eastward from Asia across Beringia into North America. The archaeological chronology is so extensive here that Onion Portage has become the standard by which all other Alaskan sites are measured.

Nowhere else in Alaska, not even at Cape Krusenstern, is the prehistoric record so complete. Unlike Krusenstern, Onion Portage is vertical: Dig down and you pass through a stack of more than 70 different artifact-bearing layers. The importance of these strata is that they firmly fix the sequence of all the different cultures at Onion Portage, and help provide relative dates as well.

After Giddings died following an auto accident in 1964, his assistant Dr. Douglas Anderson—also of Brown—took charge. Today the Onion Portage Archeological District, listed in the National Register of Historic Places, embraces 15,360 acres, mostly Native owned.

The deposits here go back at least 10,000 years—40 centuries older than Krusenstern's most ancient finds—to the Akmak culture. In Eskimo, akmaaq means "chert," the flinty rock this people used for tool and weapon blades. Similar and somewhat older blades found in Japan and Siberia bolster the evidence for contact across Beringia. Bone fragments in Alaska show that the Akmak hunted not only caribou but also large-horned bison, horses, and other beasts that soon would disappear from the continent.

Sediment studies reveal that as recently as 14,000 years ago northwestern Alaska was a patchwork of sandy desert and thinly vegetated meadow. The thousands of lakes now peppering this area did not exist then. Despite its location, the Kobuk Valley escaped glaciation in this period and became an ice-free refuge for animals and man. Massive glaciers lay farther east, locking up huge amounts of water.

There is a desert look in the Kobuk country even today; at two places just south of the Kobuk River, active sand dunes that date back at least 24,000 years still advance and ebb in a duel with the surrounding spruce forest. The sand was carried by rivers and glaciers from the Baird and Schwatka Mountains, and the Kobuk funneled it here. Winter winds from the northeast have long been shuffling the dunes westward, gradually covering forest and pushing back or swallowing streams. The opposite holds true at the sand's eastern edge, which generally is being vegetated and stabilized. Thus the active dune areas, some 25 square miles in size, are moving west, like giant amoebas. Currently they constitute a prime visitor attraction.

Since the park has no roads, getting to the dunes—or anywhere else—means either chartering a plane or boating the Kobuk and then hiking inland. River travelers can put in as far upstream as Walker Lake in the central Brooks Range, but a much closer entry to the park is the village of Ambler, about ten river miles east of Onion Portage.

One of a handful of villages on the Kobuk, Ambler dates back to the 1950s, when Eskimo families first came here. It has a pleasantly decayed feel, similar to Appalachia's, but more lush, less steep and rocky. In addition to a population of about 200, it boasts an airstrip, gravel streets, and city water.

 (Continued on page 163)

Nomads of the Arctic, caribou trail an ancient route to the Kobuk each fall. White-throated bulls, sleek from summer grazing, brandish

four-foot-long antlers. Caribou mate en route and usually winter south of the river. In spring they move north, where they calve and crop tundra plants until their Kobuk journey begins again.

*P*owerful kicks churn silver wakes as caribou surge across the Kobuk near the Onion Portage oxbow—an ancient hunting ground and one of the most important sites ever found in Arctic archaeology. Evidence of human presence here dates back 10,000 years. The tradition endures: Eskimos still hunt at Onion Portage, bagging the migrants as they swim. His boat laden, a departing hunter leaves antlers stacked at riverside. Kobuk caribou form part of the Western Arctic herd, largest in Alaska, numbering 170,000 adults.

For my Kobuk River journey I fly to Ambler with four companions, a rubber raft, and three inflatable kayaks. Anyone who has tried an inflatable kayak knows you don't get into it as much as put it on, squeezing legs and rump inside what amounts to a rubber ducky, which rides so lightly that it moves at the slightest whim of current or wind. I have a rough time finding room for my 6′3″, 205-pound frame—especially in the bow, where a gear bag competes for space. But such discomforts are more than balanced by the kayak's mobility and its low, loon's-eye view, just above the water's surface.

The river meanders; the land falls into horizontal bands of color: Beneath blue sky lies a purplish veneer of distant mountains, followed by the spruce forest's dark green, then some willows turning their autumnal yellow, a tan stripe of gravel beach, and finally the Kobuk's flat, black water. The kayaks readily respond to our paddles—until crosswinds come up and whip them about like so many weather vanes. The situation gets impossible near Onion Portage, where the river takes 180-degree bends while the wind does not. Eventually I give up trying to stay pointed downstream and just drift.

Now and then an isolated cabin appears on the riverbank. Most residents pursue traditional subsistence activities: hunting, fishing, gathering berries and other wild plants. Over the past 20 years Howard and Erna Kantner have built a home, raised a family, and found a new life-style—all on a windswept bluff in what is now the park, some 35 miles downriver from Ambler. There have been hardships, but the Kantners exude a quiet determination—and a gentle warmth, as tangible as the physical warmth of their wood-burning stove.

Howard came to Alaska in 1953 to attend college at Fairbanks. "I didn't really like Alaska at first," he admits. "It was cold, and full of those stunted trees. But each day it grew on me." He became fascinated with Eskimos. "They're a real special people," he says. "More tolerant and, well, I just enjoy being with them. For a time I lived with an elderly Eskimo couple on the coast—she was the daughter of a medicine man who had no son, so she had had to learn to hunt as a young girl. She was good, too; she taught me to hunt, and made clothes for me out of animal skins. Her husband had been an orphan, which is kind of special to Eskimos, mystical in a way. He taught me a lot of Eskimo lore. In return I hunted for them and brought in food."

Years later, Howard met Erna and they moved to the Kobuk, adopting an intensely Native life-style. They built an igloo to live in—the traditional wood-and-earth Eskimo home, half in and half out of the ground, not the ice-block domes popularized in cartoons.

With the passing years the Kantners refined their Kobuk life-style, learning by doing. A vegetable garden took root; sled dogs enabled them to haul supplies and check traplines more easily. Some years Howard needed scores of caribou in addition to other game and thousands of fish, just to feed his family and dogs. Now, because of fewer dogs and a different diet, he takes only six caribou annually.

The Kantners soon learned why Eskimos traditionally rebuilt igloos every year or two: Wood next to the ground rots rapidly, and the moss roof absorbs a lot of water, adding to the chill. Today they live in a less traditional but more enduring post-and-beam sod house, with a plywood floor instead of dirt, and a metal roof that diverts rainwater into barrels, saving them some of the drudgery of hauling drinking water uphill. Triple-insulated windows let in light but little

"We wanted to live the Eskimo way. Not own the land, just live on it." In their cabin on the Kobuk, Howard and Erna Kantner tell visitors of the quest that led them here 20 years ago. Established as local residents, they may live and hunt in the park. But weapons see less use today as the Kantners eat less meat and have fewer sled dogs to feed.

cold, and a door has replaced the hanging skins that guarded the portal of their igloo. But their basic philosophy remains unchanged. "We wanted to live the Eskimo way," Howard says. "Not own the land, just live on it. Sure, we could have staked out a homestead here, but that just didn't seem right. We're really only . . . squatters."

Under the Alaska parklands law they can stay as long as they like. Howard feels that the park's creation was a good thing. But he wishes that people "could still come up and just try it out the way we did— it's been such a special experience. Living with the land, not just off it. You learn a lot about a place—and yourself."

Just then some unexpected arrivals showed up at the Kantners' boat landing: a party of five floating the Kobuk in a raft. They sought food and shelter. It was 11:30 at night, but Erna and Howard invited the group in. Such open-door policy is common in the bush.

Only two days earlier, at Onion Portage, I had seen the same party enjoying the hospitality of park ranger Tek Kilgore, filling his cabin and eating his food. Then Tek was asked if he would use the Park Service boat to tow the rafters to Kotzebue—some 140 miles downriver. Tek explained that towing was not a service normally offered by park personnel. Were the visitors in trouble?

It turned out that the group had intended to float the Noatak River, but when bad weather kept their charter pilot from landing at its headwaters, they opted for the nearby Kobuk. They had no map of the Kobuk—which offers some challenging white water, in contrast to the flat Noatak. And they had allotted only 18 days for a trip that usually takes four weeks. But luck was with them. They survived the rapids, and the Kobuk—unlike the Noatak, which has no villages in its first 365 miles—offered a string of settlements at which food and fuel could be bought or begged. A few miles downstream from the park, the party arranged for a tow to Kotzebue.

Most park visitors, says Superintendent Mack Shaver, come better prepared. Only a very few stumble in without a realistic plan or adequate supplies and end up by seeking help or handouts. Good that such visitors are few, or else the storied hospitality of the bush might soon wear thin. And the demand might grow here, as it has elsewhere, to make the park safe with new regulations, visitor stations, and the like. Such changes would totally alter the original wild-and-free intent of Kobuk Valley.

And so, a word of caution: Do not go lightly into our Alaskan parks. The northern ones have almost no facilities. You are expected to get yourself in and out, taking all you need with you. This does not mean the parks are for the young and vigorous only—I have met 70-year-old canoeists here—but these parks are surely not for the careless.

There are rewards that come with taking the unblazed path, with going where you cannot count on others bailing you out of a tight spot. Two centuries of westward and northern expansion have greatly depleted America's wild land, yet always there was more, beyond the frontier. Not so today; although sizable pockets of wilderness remain in our western states, none can compare with the vast wilds of Alaska. Already, civilization has touched the nation's highest peaks and northernmost shores. Should public pressure ever demand that Alaska's national parks be made less wild and more developed, the transition would be technologically easy to bring about. But once the wilderness is gone from Alaska, we will have no more of its kind.

No desert mirage but a relic of the Ice Age, the Great Kobuk Sand Dunes formed from the windblown outwash of melting glaciers. Hikers trek 1½ miles from boats on the Kobuk to scale the dunes—the park's most popular attraction. Hardy grasses (below) scribe leaf prints in the sand.

FOLLOWING PAGES: With day's end comes a tranquil pause in a Kobuk journey. Easily stowed inflatable craft reduce the bulk for bush planes—and the costs to river runners. Fishing rod can reel in fresh food en route.

NOATAK

By Tom Melham

IN AGE THE TWO MEN were well into their middle years. But in mood they were a couple of kids at Christmastime. They had just arrived at a lake high in the central Brooks Range, where a hired pilot had cached canvas gear bags days before. Eagerly they tore open the bags, dumping the hinged frame and rubbery skin of a collapsible two-man boat. In quick succession they assembled the parts, test-floated the result, and packed it with four weeks' supplies.

They were about to realize an old dream—to float the entire Noatak River. Before them lay hundreds of miles of braided and winding waterway and hundreds of miles of wide-open tundra rimmed by the untrammeled Brooks Range, as this totally Arctic stream makes its way from its headwaters in the glaciers of Mount Igikpak to Kotzebue Sound. It took the two only minutes to get their boat into the infant Noatak and shove off, in pursuit of their dream.

About 400 river runners also went down the Noatak in that summer of 1982, perhaps 15 times as many as did only a decade earlier, when few outside Alaska had ever heard of this stream. Today it has become something of a legend, prized for its remoteness, its mystique, and mostly its pristine state. Although it cannot boast the Nile's length, the Colorado's canyons, or the Mississippi's volume, the Noatak flows wild and free from start to finish. No dams or levees hem it in, and only one village stands on its shores.

The Noatak rarely rages; it is not a spectacular torrent but a mood river, subtle in form and color. For most of its length it frays apart in great watery braids that merge and separate endlessly, at times splitting almost to infinity, as if it cannot decide where to go and so goes everywhere. Its celebrated Grand Canyon actually is a valley. While nearby Noatak Canyon qualifies as a canyon, the main attraction lies in solitude, not in white water. Landscapes along the river are at once stark and delicate, striking yet understated; desolate mountains and brashly sprawling tundra contradict the gentle veneers of wild flowers and the soft pastels wrought by the Arctic's magical light.

But then variety is the watchword of the Noatak basin, which embraces nearly every known type of arctic habitat. Its animal life shows remarkable variety despite the river's restrictive location 30 to 110 miles above the Arctic Circle. Noting the preponderance of caribou, wolf, wolverine, grizzly bear, and Dall's sheep, former park planner John Kauffmann envisioned the Noatak as "a sparer, arctic version of Africa's Serengeti."

Treeless realm of tundra sprawls from bog to Brooks Range heights in the eastern end of Noatak National Preserve. Tufts of cotton grass brighten its wetter areas, while fireweed (above) often sprouts in burned-over spots. Some 500 kinds of plants make the Noatak valley home to one of the most diverse assemblages of flora in the Arctic world.

Photographs by Tim Thompson

NOATAK NATIONAL PRESERVE. 6,559,000 acres. MAJOR FEATURES: 210 miles of
Noatak River cutting canyons and valleys through Brooks Range; grizzlies,
Dall's sheep, caribou; golden eagles, gyrfalcons, peregrines. FACILITIES: None.
ACCESS AND ACCOMMODATIONS: Air charters, supplies at Ambler, Kotzebue,
Bettles Field; lodging at Kotzebue, Bettles Field. ACTIVITIES: River trips,
backpacking, wildlife watching, fishing, sport hunting. FOR INFORMATION:
Superintendent, Box 287, Kotzebue, Alaska 99752.

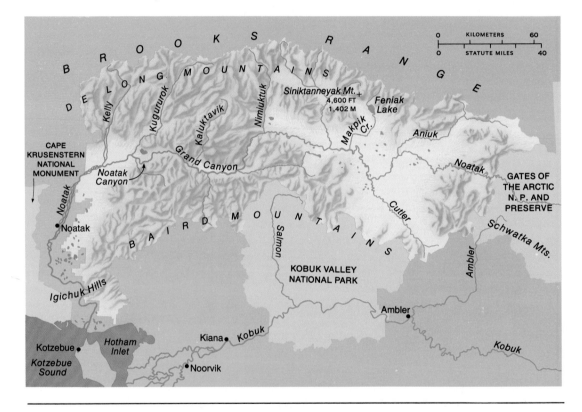

So noteworthy is this area, in fact, that Congress has not only declared almost all of the Noatak a National Wild and Scenic River, but
has also set aside the bulk of its watershed—everything between the
De Long and Baird Mountains—as Noatak National Preserve. Designation of this entire parkland as a preserve reflects its popularity
among sport hunters who covet the wild white sheep. Two sections
of the river—the uppermost and the lowermost—poke out beyond
the preserve, but the headwaters lie within the Gates of the Arctic National Park, while the lowland stretch passes through lands claimed
or owned by a Native corporation. UNESCO has designated the Noatak parkland a biosphere reserve, citing its value in scientific research and as representative of Alaskan tundra.

Noatak National Preserve spreads across more than 6.5 million
acres, yet most visitors keep to the relatively small corridor of its major river. This is partly due to the fact that there are no roads or regular tour services; getting around here in summertime means either

boating the Noatak or paying the considerable costs of air charters. Another reason is the river's celebrity status. People have heard of the Noatak, and see it as the heart of this new parkland.

Still, there is much beyond the banks of the Noatak, including areas never extensively traveled on foot in recent times—except by caribou. For photographer Tim Thompson and myself, step one in getting to such areas was to hire pilot Tom Falley and his floatplane. Step two was to set a fuel cache in the preserve, so that we could fly to the most remote niches and still come back. Tom chose Feniak Lake for its central location and cached about 150 gallons of gasoline. It cost $1,242, including transportation to Feniak, or $8.28 per gallon.

That afternoon we hiked to a nearby peak called Siniktanneyak, which had the barren and wasted feel of an old quarry. Pile after pile of bare talus slumped down toward us—until we happened upon a lone wild flower, a fuchsia-colored, five-petaled bit of perfection bursting forth bravely out of all that gray and lifeless scree. And suddenly this craggy wasteland seemed considerably less grim.

Soon it softened even more; we passed clumps of butter-yellow arctic poppies, purplish stands of fireweed—so named because it is often the first plant to take root after fires or floods bare the soil—and Siberian phlox, whose blossoms vary in color from a pale bluish white through indigo and deep violet to magenta. The calendar was a week into July, but the Arctic was still clinging to spring. There were waterfalls as well, stairstepping between pools of the clearest water I'd seen, even in Alaska. Water without a hint of the usual murk or motes, without even bubbles to obscure the bouldered bottom—or the 12-to-15-inch grayling lingering there.

We left Feniak for the preserve's eastern end, where a small, nameless lake provided us with landing strip and campsite. We woke the next morning to the splashings of some loons at play. Tom rolled out first, grabbed a fly rod, and within minutes landed a fish. It seemed rather ugly to me—blunt of head and large of paunch. Despite its looks, however, the arctic char made a delicious breakfast for us all, tastier than grayling and nearly as rich as salmon.

We lazed through morning, enjoying the vast empty feel of the valley floor. Afternoon was devoted to an uphill hike toward a double mountain about six miles away. The land's smooth curves quickly changed; outcrops of rock poked through grassy foothills like elbows through an old sweater. And although surface water remained abundant, we soon came upon landforms that could have been transplanted from America's arid Southwest. Rocky knobs, swathed with pastel bands, mimicked the Painted Desert's eroded rock. Steep canyons occasionally channeled the land, while cracked arches and pinnacles offered the bare profiles and varied tones of Grand Canyon or Bryce. Colors everywhere were muted; tawny browns and grays joined with earthy reds, greens, and purples, blushing or fading in the rarefied sunlight of the far north.

Late in the day my companions headed back to camp while I went on, intending to sleep somewhere on the mountain, scale its far side, and return through the saddle separating its twin, mile-high peaks. I agreed to meet Tom back at the lake at 2 p.m. the next day.

I bedded down that night on a mossy cushion at the Y of a stream. Although it rained, I slept well, for the clouds kept the midnight sun at bay. It took less than two hours to reach the mountain's saddle; no

_T_undra meets taiga—
northern spruce forest—
beside a lake that feeds
the Kelly River, a
Noatak tributary. In this
totally Arctic preserve
variations in drainage
and permafrost depth
produce such isolated
spruce pockets north
of the tree line. Bogs
and ponds also provide
prime breeding grounds
for the Arctic's storied
mosquitoes, which often
end up as fish food—
contributing at least
indirectly to the author's
successful quest for
northern pike (above).

amount of time, however, would have prepared me for the view it afforded. I stood at one end of a bouldered causeway walled by two fractured spires. At the far end the world dropped away, tumbling down to the glittering Noatak. Beyond lay lakes and more mountains—long, humpbacked rows of grayish green, tapering into Alaska's immense North Slope and eventually the Arctic Ocean.

While walking that causeway I chanced to look back—and saw another face watching mine. A full-curl Dall's sheep, only 50 yards away. I froze, hoping to prolong the moment. Soon my cramped body cried out and I edged back, expecting this notoriously shy beast to bolt. But he could have been a statue. For the next 20 minutes he just stood there watching me. What made him so curious? Had he never seen a man before—at least one without a gun? Probably not. But this may have been the closest he'd ever been to one, just as it was my closest—and longest—meeting with a wild sheep.

Skies were clearing, a pleasant alpine meadow lay before me—I wished every day could start out as well. Along the way I heard a sudden *kir!* overhead and looked up to see a rough-legged hawk soar and drop and rise again, riding the morning thermals. I felt pretty buoyant myself, reaching the lake in good time. That joy slowly paled, however, for Tom did not show. Was he in trouble?

Finally, around 4 o'clock I heard the buzz of his Super Cub and saw it circle down. "Sorry for the inordinate delay," sighed Tom as he tossed me a mooring line. "But somebody 'borrowed' our gas. Took all but 18 gallons." Just enough to get Tom's near-empty plane to the village of Ambler and the nearest gas. The cost of our trip had suddenly increased, but it could have been far worse. Had no gas been left, we would have been marooned—Tom at Feniak some 55 miles away, and me here. It was so incredible. We hadn't seen another person in days. And now this. I felt as if I'd been mugged in paradise.

We never found out who took our cache, or why, but the incident underlines the advice of Park Service brochures: Visitors must be ready to deal with the unexpected. Not all are. Two months later I would fly over a drowned plane in a Noatak tributary. Apparently the pilot had moored it too snugly, not allowing for fluctuations in water level; while he slept the river had risen several feet. The same floods that dunked his plane claimed the lives of two rafters on the Noatak. Such are the moods of the unpredictable stream.

Summer's endless daylight and balmy weather can lull Noatak visitors into a mistaken sense of forever, that the river is always peaceful, the tundra eternally bland. In fact, tundra is a battleground for many forms of life, besieged by both extremes: fire and ice. Year round, most of this land is frozen solid. Summer thaws only its upper skin—several inches to several feet deep. Underneath lies permafrost. Summer also brings fires—usually sparked by lightning. On occasion the fires bring scientists.

I met Dr. Peter Marchand, a plant ecologist, near the confluence of the Kugururok and Noatak Rivers, the site of several wildfires in recent years. He and his team had come from Johnson State College in Vermont to study the tundra's response to fire—measuring thaw depths and analyzing layers of soil for past environmental trends as one might examine tree rings. "It's a tough environment," Marchand said. "And much more dynamic than a lot of people think." He noted that most of its plants are perennials, which reproduce in two ways:

Brooding rockscapes give a harsh, unfinished feel to Siniktanneyak Mountain near Feniak Lake; passing clouds and occasional tarns do little to soften the image. The mountain's name, an Eskimo term, reportedly means "place where one cannot sleep." Though Native people probably hunted here, none stayed long. Today the land remains so wild that visitors still assume—mistakenly— that no other human trod here before them.

They can flower and go to seed, or they can sprout each year from underground portions of previous growth. The latter method—vegetative reproduction, or cloning—gives them a head start in the brief growing season. In contrast, annuals—plants that live just one season—cannot clone. Their sole option is to produce seed. Yet some manage to proliferate here. "Annuals are the curiosity of the arctic plant world," Marchand said. "They have only four or at most six weeks to germinate, grow, produce viable seeds, and get them out. If they don't it's 'game over' for the species."

Marchand and project leader Dr. Charles Racine think fire may help annuals compete. Fire clears established growths and chars the

"A sparer, arctic version of Africa's Serengeti," suggested a park planner of the Noatak watershed, which boasts whistling swans (above) in its seasonal showcase of Asian and North American birds; moose (opposite), Dall's sheep, wolves, grizzlies, and caribou also inhabit the Noatak parkland. Its preserve designation dictates that it remain open to sport as well as subsistence hunting.

surface, which increases absorption of sunlight and thaws the ground deeper, releasing more nutrients and making a better seedbed. Racine adds that since seeds of annuals usually are more numerous, smaller, and quicker to germinate than those of perennials, they often successfully colonize burned areas. But over time, Marchand explains, perennials tend to crowd out annuals, "until another tundra fire gives them temporary reprieve."

A given patch of tundra, says Racine, experiences a major fire every 200 or 300 years. Floods, landslides, and other events that similarly disrupt the surface also appear to favor annuals, he adds. Thus, what may be a disaster for most organisms actually helps others to compete, and so to survive in an unforgiving land.

The harsh cold and unsheltered vastness of this valley have spawned another windfall: They have preserved the area by discouraging man from living in it. Even the hardy Eskimo, who has hunted and fished here for untold generations, rarely lingers past autumn. Man's use of the region remains largely seasonal. That is not surprising. There is something alien and almost frightening about it; the awesome sweeps are too lonely, too perfectly bleak for us to dwell here permanently. But to visit this Arctic world, to explore one small piece of it and lose ourselves in its grand scale, to drink its waters and fish its rivers and forget the world of back home—if only for a moment—is the essence, the enduring lure of this land.

Splitting away only to rejoin later, a meandering spur of the Noatak severs a gravel bar in the preserve's eastern end. Throughout its 400-mile length the river tends to braid rather than tumble; its tameness and its volume have helped make it the area's major thoroughfare.

FOLLOWING PAGES: *Unfettered by the works of man, the river's midsection twists past tiny lakes and gaunt Arctic sweeps. The Noatak requires minimal boating skills but maximal planning; no towns or facilities touch its first 375 miles. Most boaters begin some 50 miles east of the preserve, flying in with 75 to 100 pounds of food and gear per person for the four-week voyage to the river's mouth.*

GATES
OF THE ARCTIC

By Tom Melham

There is something glorious in traveling beyond the ends of the earth, in living in a different world which men have not discovered, in cutting loose from the bonds of world-wide civilization. Such life holds a joy and an exhilaration. . . .
—Bob Marshall, 1934

WILDERNESS WAS HIS BATTLE CRY. A founder of the Wilderness Society, he was a forester by profession, a conservationist by conviction, and a backwoods rambler by preference. And when Bob Marshall first visited Alaska in 1929, he found what would become his favorite wilderness for life: the central Brooks Range. The fact that it then was a huge blank on the map midway between Fairbanks and Barrow, the nation's northernmost settlement, fascinated him, for he yearned to explore where others had never been. Eagerly he returned several times during the 1930s, expounding again and again on the joys of the craggy, vast, and largely unknown wilds.

Although Marshall actually was not the first to travel here, he did more to popularize the area than any predecessor. He also scaled perhaps 28 of its mountains. On one hike up the Koyukuk River he christened two nameless peaks Frigid Crags and Boreal Mountain, referring to them as "Gates of the Arctic."

All three names stuck and four decades later, when Congress first considered legislation to create a Brooks Range wilderness park, Marshall's phrase was chosen to entitle the proposal. In time Gates of the Arctic National Park and Preserve became reality.

The parkland, spanning 8.5 million acres, commands the very core of the Brooks Range. About 11 percent—the preserve portion—was left open to sport hunting. To the west of Gates sprawls the 6.6 million acres of Noatak National Preserve, while the 19-million-acre Arctic National Wildlife Refuge lies to the east. These reserves enfold almost the entire Brooks Range. Their vast size reflects not only the area's colossal natural beauty but also the desire of planners to set aside wildernesses that go beyond human scale, preserving entire watersheds and ecosystems rather than mere pieces of them.

Fifty years ago similar logic moved Bob Marshall to urge that everything north of the Yukon River—almost half of Alaska—be closed to development. The proposal died with him, and now a pipeline and haul road—to the Prudhoe Bay oil field on the Arctic Ocean—sever his beloved mountains. Even so, this 600-mile-long Arctic

How high the peaks? Totally treeless, the bleak north flank of the Brooks Range lacks visual scale. Though dusted with snow even in August, these mountains stand no more than 7,500 feet high, half a mile above the valley floor. A southern exposure supports a more varied plant life, evidenced by a highbush cranberry in fall colors and a lichen-encrusted poplar.

ABOVE: JAMES H. KATZ
OPPOSITE: BOB WALDROP

GATES OF THE ARCTIC NATIONAL PARK AND PRESERVE. 8,473,000 acres.
MAJOR FEATURES: Pristine Brooks Range country, epitomizes "the last great wilderness." Wild rivers, North Slope tundra; grizzly and black bears, wolves, Dall's sheep, caribou, moose, wolverines. FACILITIES: None. ACCESS AND ACCOMMODATIONS: Air service to Bettles Field, Anaktuvuk Pass. Air charters, lodging, supplies at Fairbanks, Bettles Field. ACTIVITIES: Backpacking, mountaineering, wildlife watching, cross-country skiing, river trips, fishing. Sport hunting in preserve. FOR INFORMATION: Superintendent, Box 74680, Fairbanks, Alaska 99707.

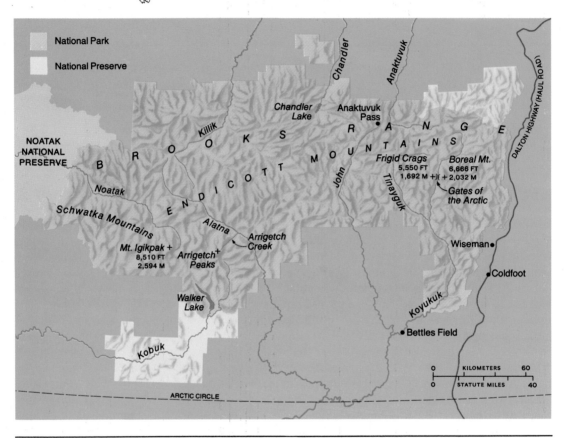

range remains North America's largest wilderness enclave, and Gates of the Arctic qualifies as one of our ultimate wilderness parks.

Gates is more vertical than neighboring Noatak, and farther from cities than Denali or Wrangell-St. Elias. It contains not a single year-round road and only one year-round village. It straddles the awesome Arctic divide, embracing the headwaters of the nation's most important Arctic rivers—the Noatak, Kobuk, and Colville—as well as the Koyukuk, Alatna, John, and many others. It is a place where caribou, Dall's sheep, bears, and wolves run in plenty, where rock walls plunge to lichen heaths and grassy tussocks, where riverbanks may be as treeless as icebergs—or thicketed with impenetrable stands of alder, willow, and birch. It is a monument to the joys of uncompromised arctic wilderness.

As such, Gates of the Arctic may not be everyone's favorite park. It surely is not for day-trippers who expect to drive from one scenic overlook to the next. Summer travel here is by plane, boat, or foot; the terrain can be extremely challenging and the remoteness argues for stays of a week or more. Primarily, this park is for veteran hikers, climbers, kayakers, and other experienced lovers of the wilds.

Yet the difficulties are compensated by incredible natural delights. The best known is called Arrigetch Peaks, or simply the Arrigetch, after the Eskimo expression that conveys a word picture of the peaks: "fingers of the hand extended." The Arrigetch is a granitic intrusion in the vast limestone barricade of the Brooks Range, and it possesses a haunting beauty that has made it a sort of gold standard for the region, an ideal against which other mountains are measured.

The Arrigetch is one of the most spectacular mountain areas I have ever seen. A dozen different valleys crease it; venture up any of them and you walk amid soaring upthrusts and startling undercuts and overhangs and knife-edged vanes—all in black granite. Giant, slightly curved rock fangs slouch in rows like so many witches' hats. Everywhere the stone exfoliates in smooth concentric layers—just as an onion sloughs off its outer skin—leaving promontories slick and without handholds. Hanging glaciers poise atop cliffs thousands of feet up, seemingly ready to crack off at any moment.

There is a dark side to the beauty here, a splintered look, a feeling that life is always on the line. But there is softness as well: Wild flowers splash their colors across grassy and lichened meadows. Hairline waterfalls trace delicately down near-vertical slopes, ending in clear lakes and lush valleys where moose and grizzlies dwell. Streams fill seasonally with grayling and with the far less noticeable sculpin that mimics streambed stones in color and shape.

Travel in the Arrigetch is often wet. During a 15-day hike there rain fell 14 days. Nearby Bettles Field averages only 11 inches of precipitation a year, but these mountains make their own weather. Good rain gear and clothing that warms even when wet are musts. Also recommended: an ability to cope with depression, moldy tents, and the other discomforts that come with rainy skies.

Then there are the mosquitoes, ever able to find a spot—under your chin, perhaps, or behind a knee—where they can settle down for dinner. Creekside thickets of alder, willow, and birch pose yet another trial. No matter how carefully you place your feet among the tangles, a wayward branch always lashes out when least expected, sending you sprawling. You get up infuriated, your anger ballooning as you see a moose stride effortlessly on its long legs, covering in minutes the half mile that took you hours of nonstop thrashing.

Sometimes the only alternative to the thickets is to hike on tussocks, which can be almost as hellish. These matted clumps of grass or sedge rise up from otherwise flat tundra. They may stand a foot or two in height, so obscured by billowy top growth that the simple act of walking becomes a complicated exercise. Hikers have two options. They can feel their way between the tussocks to ground level, which is often covered by water. Or they can try to balance atop the mounds. The trouble with the latter method is that a boot must land dead center on each tussock—or the unstable clump will twist and tilt suddenly, pitching the walker into the wet.

The physical hardships and remoteness of Gates encourage a feeling that this federally protected wilderness will remain forever wild. In fact it already bears scars; the enemy is us. Ann Odasz, a plant ecologist, has studied the human impact on this part of the Arctic for years. In 1978 it took her half a week to hike up Arrigetch Creek Valley to the Arrigetch. Now there's a trail—it takes her only a day. The trail, worn nearly a foot deep in places, was made by hikers who followed the footsteps of others before them. Although they could have taken any number of different routes to the peaks, they stuck to the creek because they had heard of it, and because it was near a lake where a floatplane could land.

They did not realize that their steps were killing the fragile carpet of lichens, compacting the soil, and increasing erosion. Once established, such paths only beckon more hikers, Ann Odasz told me, and the lichens have almost no chance to regenerate. They are slow growers even in the best of times. She pointed to a two-inch-long sprig that, she said, could take 150 years to reach full growth.

"Lichens are especially fragile in dry weather," she went on, "and I've seen people camp on them here when they're stone dry, crumbling them to talcum powder. You could tell exactly where they'd stepped and where they'd put up tents, long after they had left."

A simple cure, she added, would be for visitors to camp on sedges or grasses, which can stand far more abuse. She also advises against the traditional campfire. Campers long ago exhausted the meager supply of deadwood along the creek, and now some have turned to live spruce trees—in violation of park rules. Gnarled and twisted, often into charming candelabra shapes, these trees are scrawny enough to seem mere saplings. But in the Arrigetch a four-inch-thick tree trunk can represent 300 years of growth.

To someone who has not wandered truly wild land the sight of a trail or a campfire's charred remains may seem inconsequential. But to those who have experienced pristine wilderness these scars are an outrage. They are, after all, what people come to the Brooks Range to avoid. Ann Odasz, who knew Arrigetch Creek at its wildest, says that when she first saw the pathway "it made me feel like I was in an ordinary national park, not the boonies." She is not alone in her concern. Bob Waldrop, an outfitter who once guided groups throughout the Arrigetch, now shuns Arrigetch Creek entirely. "It's changed," he explains. "Changing more every year."

The changes are especially regrettable because they are so needless. Park officials counted some 2,600 visitors in 1983—an average of one person for every 3,000 acres. Certainly the park could absorb this number of people and more, if they were evenly dispersed. But far too many descend upon Arrigetch Creek.

"Next year we'll be flooded with visitors," said a seasonal park ranger when he heard of my plans to visit the Arrigetch Peaks—even though I would take a seldom used route. His words may exaggerate but they contain a kernel of truth. Publicity brings people. If this book does inspire some readers to take off for the Arrigetch, I hope it also encourages them to sample lesser known areas. There are other adventures at least as grand.

In fact, publicity designed to disperse visitors is being considered by the Park Service. Another option is a permit system that would limit the number of visitors at particular areas. But Park Superintendent Richard G. Ring points out that this approach could clash with Alaska's traditionally free-spirited ways: "A permit system would have quite a bureaucratic presence. It doesn't go well with what most people come here to experience."

Bursting free with a flourish, an unnamed stream in the park's northeastern corner vaults a natural rock dam, then trickles off toward the distant Arctic Ocean. Above the dam the split-level valley opens into a broad, grassy meadow bounded by the haunting silence and open-roofed architecture of the central Brooks Range.

FOLLOWING PAGES: *Fall snows and colors drape the Arrigetch country, goal of many park visitors. Tawny poplars and skinny spruces top the scrubby mix; dense growth here can cut a hiking pace of three miles an hour to one mile in three hours.*

OPPOSITE: TOM MELHAM, NATIONAL GEOGRAPHIC STAFF

FOLLOWING PAGES: J. & M. IBBOTSON/ALASKAPHOTO

A more palatable method, he feels, might be to encourage outfitters and air taxi operators—who take most visitors into the park—to guide customers away from heavily used areas. Also, the Park Service probably will distribute statements to visitors that outline ways to go easy on the fragile land—and may even list heavily used regions best left off one's wilderness itinerary.

One seemingly innocuous statement—a list indicating where different fish might be found in the Brooks Range—quickly drew fire and has been withdrawn. Roger Kaye, an environmentalist who works with conservation groups in Alaska, argued that the list unintentionally encouraged increased use of certain areas simply by naming them. The information, he said, included the sizes of fish at these places. "We feel that Gates is a place where you can discover things on your own," Kaye told me.

Bob Waldrop goes further, objecting even to giving names to the nameless topographic features in the park. Scores of names were be-

stowed by none other than Bob Marshall, who paradoxically praised blank areas on the map—and then proceeded to fill them in.

"I like the unknownness of the Brooks," says Waldrop. "You're really not sure what's over this pass or beyond that mountain. Even today many peaks and knobs still don't have names; I like that, too. When Marshall went around naming everything he saw, things he didn't even get close to, he ruined it for others. Everyone should have the chance to experience what he experienced—total wilderness."

I have taken part in two Waldrop hikes, one to a rarely visited section of the Arrigetch, the other to, well, I'd rather not say. It's a mountain that Bob Marshall named 50 years ago, but in the spirit of Waldrop and Kaye, I don't want to endanger it with publicity.

This mountain sits in the northern part of Gates. Part of the mountain and one side of the valley leading to it have been uplifted and eroded into row upon row of triangular projections, like fish scales. The feel here is very different from that of the Arrigetch; colors are subtle, the rock is layered limestone, and the land's lack of trees leaves it without any scale. Foothills might be thousands or only hundreds of feet high. It was like a mirage—toying with your senses, seeming to go in and out of focus, pulsing in and out of reality.

We took nearly two weeks to circle the mountain, following valleys that flanked its base, crossing from one to the next by scaling mile-high ridges. We also made side trips up glaciers, across snow bowls, and to alpine lakes. We saw Dall's sheep, caribou, and bears.

The day after we completed our circle tour, I woke early, tugged on some warming layers—in mid-August it was 22°F—and headed up a side valley. On the map it pointed like a great finger toward something I'd seen nearly every day but hadn't yet approached: the mountain's peak. The valley soon steepened into a 300-foot-high plug of limestone that sealed off its inner reaches. A small waterfall streamed down the plug's left side, turning and twisting along this rock chute, storming out of its stony prison near the bottom.

Why climb? friends sometimes ask. Why put up with the cramps and chafes of a pack, the strain and sweat and the bugs? Why endure weeks of rain and tasteless freeze-dried food? Why do things the hard way, when the airplane you charter to get there will go far higher and give even broader views?

But not this view. It took only a few minutes to scale the rock plug and enter an inner valley, one side spiked with cathedral spires, the other armored with more rows of triangular fish scales. Between lay a tawny meadow cut by meandering streams; a ewe and lamb browsed amid incomparable stillness.

I followed this timeless valley its few miles, eventually crossing a series of ridges and reaching the mountain's very summit, a rock knob just north of the Arctic divide. From here I could see 50, perhaps 100 miles in every direction, maybe more. I thought I saw the Arctic Ocean—at least I saw well down the North Slope, to where this flat land grows so dappled with the blue of lakes and lagoons that it seems half water. Behind me the entire width of the Brooks Range wrinkled along from peak to peak and from horizon to horizon. Sharp jags alternated with mesas, layer cake mountains, and other wild shapes. This was a rugged land with no hint of man, just nature, pure and free. Why climb it?

Why, indeed.

Fragile pioneers of the plant world, lichens (left) can survive even Arctic extremes by invading the slightest fissures in rock and leaching its minerals. But lichens, a living partnership of algae and fungi, grow with glacial slowness; in dry times they can succumb to a single footfall. Left undisturbed, they eventually spawn a minisoil rich enough for mosses (far left) and a succession of more complex plants.

Untitled scenics: Snowbound peaks and an ice-rimmed pond in the park's northern end (opposite) share more than intense cold with a rocky snag of the Arrigetch (left): None bear official names, an aspect applauded as fitting for the nation's ultimate wilderness park. A single year-round settlement dots the 8.5 million acres— the Native village of Anaktuvuk Pass, with some 200 residents.

FOLLOWING PAGES: Evening storm veils a ridge just north of the Arctic divide. Aircraft may provide access, but backpacking offers the best route to rugged beauty such as this.

J. & M. IBBOTSON/ALASKAPHOTO. OPPOSITE: TOM MELHAM, NATIONAL GEOGRAPHIC STAFF. FOLLOWING PAGES: BOB WALDROP

Notes on Contributors

CYNTHIA RUSS RAMSAY and TOM MELHAM, the principal authors of this book, are senior staff writers whose work appears frequently in Special Publications. In 1924 MARGARET E. MURIE became the first woman graduate of the college that is today the University of Alaska; in 1983 she became the first woman to receive the Sierra Club's highest honor, the John Muir Award. Her home is in Moose, Wyoming, within view of the Grand Tetons. The photographic team assigned to this project consisted of free lances GEORGE HERBEN, of Anchorage, Alaska; JAMES H. KATZ, of Bolinas, California; STEPHEN J. KRASEMANN, of South Gillies, Ontario; JAMES A. SUGAR, of Mill Valley, California, who also wrote a chapter; and TIM THOMPSON, of Bainbridge Island, Washington.

Additional Reading

The first expedition organized by the National Geographic Society explored Mount St. Elias in 1890, and across the decades the Society has made available a trove of information about Alaska. Check the cumulative index. Valuable background for this book was also found in the Alaska Geographic Society's quarterly publications, especially those on national interest lands and the Kotzebue Basin. Of the many other references consulted the most helpful were: Alaska Natural History Association, *This Last Treasure;* Robert H. Armstrong, *A Guide to the Birds of Alaska;* William D. Boehm, *Glacier Bay;* William O. Field,

ed., *Mountain Glaciers of the Northern Hemisphere,* vol 2; J. Louis Giddings, *Ancient Men of the Arctic;* Robert F. Griggs, *The Valley of Ten Thousand Smokes;* David M. Hopkins et al., eds., *Paleoecology of Beringia;* Bernard R. Hubbard, *Cradle of the Storms;* Sam Keith, *One Man's Wilderness;* Robert Marshall, *Alaska Wilderness;* John McPhee, *Coming into the Country;* Margaret E. Murie, *Two in the Far North;* Donald J. Orth, *Dictionary of Alaska Place Names;* Lidia L. Selkregg, ed., *Alaska Regional Profiles,* 6 vols.; Peggy Wayburn, *Adventuring in Alaska;* Frederick Hadleigh West, *The Archaeology of Beringia;* and Helen A. White, ed., *The Alaska-Yukon Wild Flowers Guide.*

Acknowledgments

From advance planning to completion of the project the Special Publications Division enjoyed the cooperation of the superintendents and staffs of the parklands. We also received important guidance from the Board of Geographic Names, the U. S. Geological Survey, the Geophysical Institute of the University of Alaska, and the Smithsonian Institution. Many of the individuals who helped us are cited in the book; in addition special thanks are owed to Robert Belous, Donald Caukins, Robert C. Cunningham, Fred Dean, Carolyn L. Driedger, Keith Gardner, Paul Haertel, David M. Hopkins, A. Durand Jones, Thomas P. Miller, David E. Moore, Stanwyn G. Shetler, Vic Van Bellenberghe, and Stephen B. Young.

INDEX

Boldface page numbers indicate illustrations.
Italicized page numbers indicate illustration captions.

Once the target of bounty hunters in Alaska, the bald eagle today enjoys the bountiful sanctuary of the national parklands. In 1982 the state provided more. To prevent logging of choice habitat, Alaska created a 48,000-acre bald eagle preserve.

Library of Congress CIP Data
Main entry under title:

Alaska's magnificent parklands.

Bibliography: p.
Includes index.
1. National parks and reserves—Alaska. 2. Parks—Alaska. 3. Alaska—Description and travel—1981-
I. National Geographic Society (U. S.)
F910.5.A38   1984   917.98   83-25036
ISBN 0-87044-442-5 (regular edition)
ISBN 0-87044-447-6 (library edition)

Composition for *Alaska's Magnificent Parklands* by National Geographic's Photographic Services, Carl M. Shrader, Director, Lawrence F. Ludwig, Assistant Director. Printed and bound by Holladay-Tyler Printing Corp., Rockville, Md. Color separations by the Lanman Progressive Co., Washington, D.C.; Lincoln Graphics, Inc., Cherry Hill, N.J.; NEC, Inc., Nashville, Tenn.; Sterling Regal, Inc., New York, N.Y.

STEPHEN J. KRASEMANN/DRK PHOTO